THE INDIAN COOKERY BOOK

THE INDIAN COOKERY BOOK

A PRACTICAL HANDBOOK TO THE KITCHEN IN INDIA,

ADAPTED TO THE THREE PRESIDENCIES;

CONTAINING

ORIGINAL AND APROVED RECIPES IN EVERY DEPARTMENT OF INDIAN COOKERY;

RECIPES FOR SUMMER BEVERAGES AND HOME-MADE LIQUEURS; MEDICINAL AND OTHER RECIPES;

TOGETHER WITH A VARIETY OF THINGS WORTH KNOWING

BY

A THIRTY-FIVE YEARS, RESIDENT

GYAN

Published by

GYAN

Gyan Publishing House
5, Ansari Road
Daryaganj, New Delhi-110002
Phone: 011-47034999, 9811692060
E-mail: books@gyanbooks.com

Distribution Network
gyanbooks.com
India, USA, Canada, UK, Australia, France

ISBN : 978-81-212-9804-9 (PB)
First Published, 1880

2nd Impression 2023

Printed at: Gyan Press, Delhi.

THE INDIAN COOKERY BOOK
Author: A THIRTY-FIVE YEARS RESIDENT

THE

INDIAN COOKERY BOOK:

A

Practical Handbook to the Kitchen in India,

ADAPTED TO THE THREE PRESIDENCIES;

CONTAINING

ORIGINAL AND APPROVED RECIPES IN EVERY DEPARTMENT OF INDIAN COOKERY;

RECIPES FOR SUMMER BEVERAGES AND HOME-MADE LIQUEURS;

MEDICINAL AND OTHER RECIPES;

TOGETHER WITH A VARIETY OF THINGS WORTH KNOWING.

BY

A THIRTY-FIVE YEARS' RESIDENT.

1880.

CONTENTS.

INTRODUCTION.

OBSERVATIONS ON THE KITCHEN AND ITS REQUIREMENTS.

THE kitchen should be roomy, light, and airy, with contrivances, in the shape of shelves and other conveniences, for laying out in order all utensils and other necessaries inseparable from the kitchen.

The oven and all the fireplaces should be constructed of fire-bricks, and not of the ordinary clay-bricks so generally used in Indian kitchens, requiring constant repairs, to the great annoyance of the cook and hindrance to his work.

A good supply of reservoirs or large earthen jars (*jallahs*) for fresh water is essential. Of these there should be two at least, both to contain equally good clean water, but yet to be applied to two widely different purposes,—the one for washing, and the other exclusively for cooking the victuals. Those who can afford the expense ought to have a reservoir on the terrace of the kitchen, and the water brought down by means of a pipe, with cock attached; which would effectually prevent dirty and greasy hands being put into the reservoirs.

The drainage should be well constructed, with a sufficient incline to carry away easily all washings and offal; and the doors and windows provided with finely-made bamboo chicks, to keep out the flies, which at some seasons are more troublesome than at others.

Great cleanliness is necessary throughout the kitchen: the flooring as well as the ceiling, the walls, and every nook and corner, ought to be kept constantly in familiar acquaintance with the whisk, and the knight of the broom called in occasionally to aid the cook in the work of a thorough turn-over. There are very many kitchens in India the ceilings of which are cleaned only once in three years, when the triennial repairs to the premises oblige it to be done.

The very best recipes, however, for ensuring a perfectly clean kitchen, well-tinned utensils, and fresh water, are the frequent visits of the lord and lady of the mansion to the cook. On these occasions expressions of satisfaction should never be withheld, if deserved, at the mode of cooking or serving up; where not merited, the one or more instances should be particularized, and such modification as may appear necessary be gradually suggested. Attention should next be directed to the order and cleanliness of the kitchen, &c.: let there be no sparing of praise, if well deserved,—such treatment is encouraging; and then, if need be, anything disorderly or unclean can be pointed out more as a passing remark than as one of complaint or censure.

UTENSILS, ETC.

THE following implements are necessary in every kitchen; and in describing them, care has been taken to use terms generally understood by the native cooks, servants, and bazaar shopkeepers, in order that young housekeepers may the more easily comprehend the requirements of the cook, and provide them accordingly:—

One curry-stone and muller.
An iron fish-kettle or ham-boiler, without the aid of which large joints, such as briskets and rounds, cannot be boiled.
An iron enamelled digester, with patent top, for soups and boiling small joints, &c.
A set of four copper stewpans, with covers.
Two large iron kettles for boiling water in, with cocks to draw off.
Two small ones for ditto, without cocks.
A copper one for serving up hot water at the table.
A set of three copper fryingpans of sizes.
One pancake ditto.
A good gridiron, with wells and drains.
One cocoanut scraper, or *narial-ka-khoornee.*
Two iron spits, or *seiks*, for roasting meats, &c.
An iron pestle and mortar.
A brass ditto.
A marble ditto.
An iron stove, or *ungatlee.*
Half a dozen iron wire dish-covers.
A good English chopper.
A *khoralee*, or an axe for cutting wood.
A butcher's knife.
Two cook-room knives.
Half a dozen common steel forks.
Half a dozen metal spoons.
Half a dozen small plated skewers for curry.
A dozen wooden spoons.
Two dal churns, or *ghootnees.*
Half a dozen palm-leaf fans.
Two common baskets and two brooms.
Four *phooknees*, or blow-pipes.
A couple of common reed mats.
A fire-poker, pincers, and shovel.
Three copper *degchees*, for boiling milk, rice, custard, &c.
One iron preserving-pan.
One copper ditto.
Half a dozen perforated bowls or colanders of sizes.
Half a dozen copper-plated pie and pudding dishes of sizes.
Half a dozen jelly-moulds of sizes.
Pepper, salt, cayenne, and flour dredging castors.
One dozen patty-pans.
Larding pins of sizes.
Nutmeg, bread, and vegetable graters, coffee-mill and coffee-roaster.
Perforated ladles of sorts.
A salting-tub, of which there are two kinds—one made of staves and iron hooped, and the other scooped out of one block of wood.
A large square board of fine or close grained wood, for rolling pastry, and two rolling-pins.
A kitchen table, and a couple of wooden stools for sitting at the table.
A set of scales and weights.
A meat-safe.
An *almirah*, or cupboard to lock up small articles.

A good supply of enamelled plates, soup-plates, and bowls for kitchen purposes, as a preventive against the necessity of using portions of dinner, breakfast, and tea services of china and porcelain. If enamelled articles are not procurable, the commonest descriptions of Spode's or Queen's ware will do, as well as the most expensive wares.

The cook should be kept well supplied with dusters, of the commonest kind, for cleaning and wiping pots and pans, and two dozens of a better, yet coarse description, for straining soups, gravy, &c.

There ought always to be a supply of twine for tying up roast meats, &c.

A quarterly reckoning should be taken of all the kitchen property in charge of the cook; this is more particularly necessary in houses where there are frequent changes of cooks and servants.

Finally, one other suggestion is of no little importance, viz., cats, dogs, and sweepers, as a rule, have no business in the kitchen. The sweeper, or, as he is elsewhere called, the "knight of the broom," should only be admitted either before the operations of the day have commenced, or after their final termination. Ninety-nine sweepers out of a hundred know that intrusions in the kitchen are against all established rule throughout the length and breadth of India; and yet, if the master or mistress be indifferent, not only the knight, but his lady also will indulge their fingers in many a savoury pie. It is no uncommon thing to find them constantly in kitchens of houses of gentlemen ignorant of the rule, peeling potatoes, shelling peas, and performing other offices for the cook, in expectation of some return for such assistance or service rendered.

TINNING OF COPPER UTENSILS.—Copper utensils are at all times preferable, but the greatest possible care must be observed in seeing that they be perfectly and thoroughly tinned every fortnight or three weeks, or at least once every month.

FUEL.—Coal should be used for all purposes of cooking, excepting only for boiling large and heavy joints of meat, requiring many hours of a steady flaming fire.

COOKS.—Never quarrel with a good cook if his only fault be that of eating from your kitchen; all cooks will do so, and a good one will eat no more than a bad one.

COINAGE AND WEIGHTS AND MEASURES.

FOR all practical purposes of this work it is not necessary to enter into any lengthened tables of the Indian weights and measures in general daily use in sale and delivery of commodities. Nor is it necessary to do more than to state in a few words the different coins current in the Indian markets.

COINAGE.

Although the introduction of the half-pice, a small copper coin, has partially superseded the use of shells called *cowries,* yet they are in daily use, for the payment of fractional parts of a pice, not only by poor natives, but also by servants on behalf of their masters, dwelling in princely mansions in the city and town of Calcutta. It is not unusual to see on tables groaning with viands the most costly a few unpretending fresh green chilies in a small glass urn with water, particularly on breakfast tables, the actual cost of which never exceeded one gunda or four cowries.

The Indian money table is computed thus:—

4 cowries make 1 gunda.
5 gundas make 1 pice.
4 pice make 1 anna.
2 annas are the eighth of a rupee.
4 annas are the quarter of a rupee
8 annas are the half of a rupee.
16 annas make one rupee.

The copper coins are of three degrees—the half-pice, the pice, and the double-pice.

There are four degrees of silver coin, the two-anna piece, the four-anna piece, the eight-anna piece, and the rupee.

It is not necessary to remark on the gold coin; but some valuable suggestions may be offered in dealing with Government of India notes in the Calcutta bazaars. The shopkeepers and poddars, as a rule, require a signature endorsed on the note before accepting it in payment of an account, or exchanging it for silver. This should be resisted in every instance; but if from any cause you are obliged to comply with the only condition on which the note will be accepted, never omit to insert, under the name, distinctly in ink, the date of endorsement: by the observance of this simple precaution, you prevent the possibility of the annoyance of being unnecessarily subjected to examination and inquiry in the event of the note being stolen subsequently to your having parted with it.

WEIGHTS AND MEASURES.

Bazaar Weights, Dry Measure.

5 sicca weight	make	1 chittack.
16 chittacks		1 seer.
5 seers		1 pusseree.
40 seers or 8 pusserees		1 maund.

Bazaar Weights, Liquid Measure.

5 sicca weight	make	1 chittack.
4 chittacks		1 pow.
4 pows		1 seer.
5 seers		1 pusseree.
40 seers or 8 pusserees		1 maund.

The following are the different weights made use of in Bengal, with their value in sicca weights:—

80 sicca weight	make	1 Calcutta bazaar seer.
80 " "		1 Serampore seer.
82 " "		1 Hooghly seer.
84 " "		1 Benares seer.
96 " "		1 Lucknow seer.
84 " "		1 Mirzapore seer.
96 " "		1 Allahabad seer.
72 sicca weight, 11 annas, 2 puns, 10 gundas, cow. 76 dec.		1 Calcutta factory seer.

Grain Measure.

5 chittacks = 1 coonkee.
4 coonkees or 20 chittacks = 1 raik or 1¼ seer.
4 raiks or 5 seers = 1 pally or pusseree.
8 pallies = 1 maund.
20 pallies = 1 soally or 2½ maunds.
16 soallies = 1 khahoon or 40 maunds.

British Indian Weights.	English Troy Weights.			
	lb.	oz.	dwt.	grs.
One maund makes	100	0	9	0
One seer "	2	6	0	0
One chittack "	—	1	17	12
One tola "	—	—	7	12
One masha "	—	—	—	15
One ruttee "	—	—	—	1,875

The articles of rice, sugar, ghee, curry condiments, poultry, salt, and other non-perishable articles are procurable all the year round, and may be purchased at all times of the day or night; but it is not so with meat, fish, and game, or with fruit and vegetables; there are seasons for these, and when in season, if not procured betimes in the morning, the chances are ten to one that all the arrangements for that day's meals will be sadly disorganized. Another inconvenience is experienced by some families ordering a particular description of fish or vegetable which is really not in season. The order is frequently misunderstood by the servant, who procures an article widely different from that ordered, or he returns empty-handed, with the declaration of the truth, "*Piah neigh,*" or "*Millah neigh,*" which means, "Could not get," or "Could not find." In order, therefore, to obviate these disappointments and inconveniences, it is deemed desirable to give a list of such articles of consumption as are procurable monthly in the Calcutta daily markets before proceeding further with other matters.

KITCHEN CALENDAR.

THE following is a list of such articles of consumption as are procurable monthly in the Calcutta daily bazaar :—

JANUARY.

Green peas, cauliflowers, cabbages, turnips, yams, potatoes, carrots, spinach, greens, cucumbers, radishes, cellery, lettuces, young onions, knol-khole, kochoo, French beans, seam, brinjals, red and white beet, &c., are in perfection and plentiful.

Beef, mutton, veal, lamb, pork, kid, poultry, &c., are also plentiful and of the first quality.

Game in great abundance—snipe, duck, teal, &c.

The fish market is well found with beckty, moonjee, rowe, cutlah, quoye, sowle, selliah, bhola, eels, banspattah, &c.

The fruits in season are Sylhet oranges, loquats, plantains, pine-apples, sugar-canes, country almonds, limes, and tipparee.

FEBRUARY.

The fish market this month has the addition of the small hilsa. Meat and vegetables continue good and abundant.

The additional vegetables are asparagus, pumpkins, and young cucumbers; and custard-apples, mulberries, bail, and small water-melons are added to the fruit.

MARCH.

The meat market continues good to about the end of this month.

Fish in abundance, with the addition of the goonteah, a small and well-flavoured fish.

Green peas and turnips disappear; salad, cabbage, carrots, and celery are on the decline; but asparagus and potatoes continue excellent; green mangoes and unripe footee are to be had, also amrah, greens, water-cresses, and the kerrella.

Fruit is also plentiful; large water-melons appear during the month, and continue in perfection for two or three months.

APRIL.

This is an unfavourable month for meat, which begins to be flabby and poor, fat, spongy, and yellow; indeed, very little good of any description is to be found in the market.

The fish market has the addition of carp, the mhagoor, and the mangoe-fish, so called from its annual visit to all the Bengal rivers at this season to spawn. This latter fish appears as soon as the mangoe is formed on the tree, and disappears at the close of the season—that is, about the middle of July. It has, perhaps, the most agreeable flavour of any in the known world, and is so sought after (by natives as well as Europeans) that, although not so large as a middle-sized whiting, it is sold at the beginning of the month at from four to eight per rupee. Before the end of May, as it becomes plentiful, the price is one rupee the score; and in June from two to three scores are sold for one rupee.

Potatoes, asparagus, onions, cucumbers, and a few cabbage-sprouts are the only vegetables procurable.

Water-melons and musk-melons are in perfection; green mangoes for pickling, and caraunda for tarts, are in great abundance.

MAY.

Grapes of the largest size, peaches, pine-apples, limes, rose-apples, lichees, jumrules, and wampees, together with water-melons, musk-melons, pomegranates, and custard-apples, come in during this month.

The meat market is very inferior to that of last month.

Fish continues good and abundant, the beckty excepted, which becomes scarce. Mangoe-fish are in great perfection this month.

Asparagus, potatoes, and cabbage-sprouts, with indifferent turnips, sweet potatoes, cucumbers, and onions, are nearly all the vegetables now in the market; pumpkins and other cucurbitaceous roots are, however, procurable.

JUNE.

Meat, as must be expected, is very indifferent this month.

The fish market is much the same as that of last month.

Mangoes and mangoe-fish are in great abundance. The Maldah mangoes arrive in Calcutta, and are considered the best that can be procured in Bengal. Grapes, peaches, lichees, &c., disappear. Custard-apples, pine-apples, jack-fruits, and guavas are in perfection.

Asparagus, potatoes, onions, and Indian corn are the principal vegetables that remain.

JULY.

Meat continues lean and poor.

The fish market continues good. The moonjee, the rowe, the cutla, the quoye, the sowle, the mhagoor, the chingree, the tangra, and the chunah are procurable all the year round. The hilsa or sable-fish makes its appearance this month: this fish is delicious, boiled, baked, or roasted, but very unwholesome. On being cured with tamarind it forms a good substitute for the herring: it is then known by the appellation of the tamarind fish.

Mangoes and mangoe-fish disappear this month.

Pine-apples, custard-apples, jacks, and guavas continue in season.

The vegetable market is very indifferent: asparagus is in season, but potatoes become poor and watery. Young lettuces, cucumbers, and sweet potatoes are now procurable; also cumrunga and caraunda.

AUGUST.

The meat and fish markets look much the same as those of last month.

Pumplenose (shaddock) appears this month; pine-apples, custard-apples, and guavas continue in perfection.

The vegetables procurable are salad, asparagus, cucumbers, brinjalls, muckun-seam (a kind of French beans), radishes, turnips, cabbage-sprouts, and some indifferent potatoes; Indian corn, cucumbers, and spinach are to be had all the year round, but are tasteless, except at this season, when they become firm, good, and palatable.

The avigato pear is sometimes procurable at this period.

SEPTEMBER.

The meat market does not improve.

The fish market experiences but slight improvement; for although there is abundance, yet it is not always firm and good, except the beckty, which becomes larger and better flavoured. The following are also in the market:—The bholia, dessy tangra, gonteah, bhengris, gontorah, kwetoonte, pyrah chanda, and the shell-fish (bagda chingree).

Vegetables are very indifferent; yams come into season about this time.

In the fruit market small oranges make their appearance; custard-apples, pine-apples, guavas, and pumplenose continue in season.

OCTOBER.

The meat market begins to revive, and the fish market to improve; the beckty becomes firm, and the others proportionably good; snipes make their appearance.

Vegetables and fruit continue much the same as last month; but if the season be favourable, both experience a considerable improvement about the end of the month.

Oranges become large and better flavoured, and custard-apples are in great perfection.

Young potatoes sometimes make their appearance this month; pomegranates are procurable, also kutbail.

NOVEMBER.

The meat market looks wholesome; beef, mutton, veal, pork, and poultry become firm and good.

Game comes in also in considerable quantities—wild duck snipes, teal, &c.

Abundance of fish is procurable, such as beckty, banspattah, gontorah, mirgal, carp, and mangoe-fish without roes.

The vegetable market begins with the introduction of green peas, new potatoes, lettuces, greens of various kinds, spinach, radishes, and turnips.

In the fruit market may be had oranges, lemons, pumplenose, custard-apples, papias, plantains, cocoanuts, country almonds, pomegranates, kutbail, &c.

DECEMBER.

The meat and fish markets are in great perfection, both as to quantity and quality; game of all kinds in abundance. The vegetable market is excellent, yielding green peas, young potatoes, lettuces, young onions, radishes, small salad, sweet potatoes, French beans, seams, brinjals, yams, carrots, turnips, greens, young cabbages, and cauliflowers. The fruit market continues much the same as last month; tipparee or Brazil currants make their appearance this month, together with wood-apples and other fruits.

THE

INDIAN COOKERY BOOK.

RICE OR CHOWL.

Rice is consumed by most European families at breakfast, tiffin, and dinner. It is eaten at breakfast with fried meat, fish, omelet, country captain, or some other curried dish, and, being invariably followed by toast and eggs, jams, fruit, &c., one *coonkee,* which contains about as much as an ordinary breakfast-cup, or say half a pound, will always be ample for four tolerably hearty consumers. There are two sizes of *coonkees,* large and small: reference is here made to the *small coonkee,* well filled. The quantity, however, of raw rice for a party of four should not exceed half a pound.

The rice at dinner is usually preceded by soup, fish, roast, and made dishes.

The best or generally approved qualities of rice for table use are known as the bhaktoolsee, the banafool, the bassmuttee, and cheenee-suckur. In purchasing these, or indeed any other approved quality, care must be taken to avoid *new rice* and what is called *urruah,* which latter has been put through some process of boiling, or damped, and then dried. Both are considered unwholesome for general daily consumption, and few Indians will use them.

Good rice when rubbed in the palm of the hand, and cleared of dust, will appear of a bright and nearly transparent yellowish colour; whereas the *urruah* will be found of a dull whitish hue, and the grain streaked and speckled with white powder, which crumbles on the application of a needle's point.

The price of rice, like other commodities, varies according to its plenty or scarcity in the market. After the cyclone of October, 1864, and again of November, 1867, the price of the bhaktoolsee and the banafool, which are fine, large, stout-grain rice, without being coarse, ruled at from eight to nine seers per rupee, and the bassmuttee and the cheeneesuckur at from seven to eight seers per rupee. The rice used by the poorer classes of the native population is of a very coarse description and incredibly cheap: within six weeks after the cyclone of November, 1867, it was readily procurable at twenty-five to thirty seers per rupee.

Rice is used in a variety of forms: it is boiled, made into kitcheeree, pellow, puddings, blanc mange, cakes, bread, &c.

The bhaktoolsee, the banafool, and other stout-grain rice are the best adapted for boiling. Boiled rice is called *bhath.*

The bassmuttee, cheeneesuckur, and all small and fine-grain rice are selected for kitcheeree, pellow, and puddings for children's food, and for invalids.

The *urruah* is used in some houses in ignorance, but for the most part it is made into flour, and used for blanc mange, cakes, &c. The flour is abundantly procurable in the Calcutta markets, and is largely used by all native bakers in the making of bread.

Twenty-two to twenty-five seers of rice monthly, consuming it three times a day, entertainments included, will be ample for a party of four, allowing occasionally for a rice pudding.

It is necessary to wash rice thoroughly in several waters before using it, and a colander is very useful for draining away the water after washing the rice.

1.—Boiled Rice.

Wash half a pound or a coonkeeful of rice, and put it to boil in a large quantity of water, over a brisk fire. Immediately the rice begins to boil, the water will bubble up to the surface of the pot and overflow, carrying away quantities of scum and impurities. The cover of the pot should now be kept partially open, and the rice stirred to prevent an entire overflow of the water. On the subsiding of the water or the bubbling, the fire should be reduced, until it is satisfactorily ascertained that the grains of rice, without being pappy, are quite soft, when the pot should be removed from the fire and a quart of cold water be added. All the liquid, which is "conjee," should then be drained, and the pot replaced over a gentle charcoal heat, to allow all moisture to evaporate, assisting the process by occasionally shaking the pot, or stirring its contents gently with a wooden spoon. Time to boil: half an hour.

The coonkee of rice when properly boiled will fill a good-sized curry or vegetable dish. The rice will be found quite soft, and yet every grain perfectly separate. Rice should never be cooked into a pap, excepting it is required for very young children; and leaving the grains hard or uncooked should be equally avoided.

A small pinch of pounded alum or *fitkerree* is used by some cooks with advantage to improve the whiteness of boiled rice.

2.—Rice Conjee.

The water in which rice is boiled should never be thrown away: it is nutritious and fattening for all cattle, horses included, and may be given daily to milch cows and goats with great advantage.

3.—Rice Kheer.

This is occasionally served upon the breakfast-table as a treat, but few Europeans care for it. It is made as follows:—Thoroughly boil one coonkee or half a pound of the bassmuttee or the cheeneesuckur rice, then drain the water away, add two cups of pure cow's milk, and put over a slow fire. As the rice begins to absorb the milk, two or three small sticks of cinnamon are put in, with one tablespoonful and a half to two tablespoonfuls of fine-quality white sugar. On the milk being entirely absorbed, the kheer is either turned out upon a dish and eaten hot, or put into a buttered mould, served up in shape, and eaten cold.

Kheer is sometimes cooked or boiled in milk only, but the foregoing recipe is supposed to be that more generally approved.

4.—Pish-Pash.

Pick and wash in several waters a coonkee or half a pound of the bassmuttee or other fine-grain rice; add to it, cleaned and cut up, a chicken, some sliced ginger, sliced onions, a few bay-leaves, some peppercorns, a few hotspice, a dessertspoonful of salt, one chittack or two ounces of butter, and water sufficient to cover the whole. Simmer over a slow fire until the chicken becomes perfectly tender and the rice quite pappy. Serve up hot. This is considered a most excellent and nutritious meal for invalids.

KITCHEEREES.

THESE are occasionally substituted for boiled rice at breakfast, and are eaten with fried fish, omelets, croquets, jhal freezee, &c. They are prepared as follows:—

5.—Bhoonee Kitcheeree.

Take rather more than three-quarters of a coonkee of bassmuttee or cheeneesuckur and half a coonkee of dal; or, if preferred, take the rice and dal in equal parts.

Take twelve large curry onions and cut them up lengthways into fine slices. Warm up two chittacks or four ounces of ghee (but before doing so be careful to warm the pot), and, while bubbling, throw in the sliced onions, removing them immediately they become of a bright brown colour. Set the fried onions aside, and throw in the dal and rice (having previously allowed all the water in which they were washed to drain through a colander). Fry until the dal and rice have absorbed all the ghee; then add a few slices of green ginger, some peppercorns, salt to taste (say one dessertspoonful), a few cloves, three or four cardamoms, half a dozen bay-leaves, and as many small sticks of cinnamon. Mix well together; add as much water only as will entirely cover over the whole of the rice and dal, put a good-fitting cover on, and set over a slow fire, reducing the same from time to time as the water is being absorbed. Care must be taken not to allow the kitcheeree to burn, which may be prevented by occasionally shaking the pot, or stirring its contents with a wooden spoon.

Serve up quite hot, strewing over it the fried onions, which serve both as a relish and garnish of the dish.

6.—Bhoonee Kitcheeree of the Mussoor or Red Dal

Is made according to recipe No. 5.

7.—Bhoonee Kitcheeree of the Moong or Small-grain Yellow Dal

Is made according to recipe No. 5.

8.—Bhoonee Kitcheeree of the Gram or Chunna Dal.

The chunna or gram dal makes a very nice kitcheeree; but, as it is rather hard, it should be boiled or soaked in cold water for an hour or so before frying it with the raw rice.

9.—Bhoonee Kitcheeree of Green Peas.

Kitcheeree made of green peas grown of English seeds is a rarity. Large peas should be picked out and shelled; they should not be fried with the rice, but added to it when nearly cooked. The instructions given in recipe No. 5 are to be observed in all other respects.

10.—Jurrud or Yellow-tinted Kitcheeree.

Jurrud or yellow-tinted kitcheeree is nothing more than one of the above kitcheerees, to which is added, at the time of frying the rice and dal, either a small quantity of saffron or turmeric, according to the colour desired to be imparted. Such introduction in no way affects the flavour, nor does it render the appearance of the dish more attractive, but serves admirably as a variety for a large breakfast-table.

11.—Geela Kitcheeree.

This is usually made of moong dal with less than one-fourth the quantity of ghee allowed for the bhoonee, or with no ghee at all, and little or no condiments are used, excepting a small quantity of finely-sliced green ginger, a few peppercorns, one or two bay-leaves, and salt to taste. It is supposed to be better adapted than bhoonee kitcheeree for children and invalids.

By *bhoonee* is meant crisp, and *geela* signifies soft.

PELLOW OR POOLOO.

Pellows are purely Hindoostanee dishes. There are several kinds of pellow, but some of them are so entirely of an Asiatic character and taste that no European will ever be persuaded to partake of them. It is therefore considered useless to offer instructions how to prepare such as the *ukhnee pellow*, in which are introduced cream, milk, butter-milk, garlic, and lime-juice; or the *sweet pellow*, in which almonds and raisins are introduced, in addition to sugar, &c.

The following are the pellows in general use:—

12.—Chicken Pellow.

Take a good-sized chicken; clean, truss, and boil it with one pound of beef in two cupfuls of clean water, seasoning it with onions, ginger, and salt. When sufficiently cooked, but yet quite firm, remove the chicken, and set it and the gravy aside. Cut up twelve onions lengthways into fine slices. Warm your pot; then melt in it two chittacks or four ounces of ghee, and, as it bubbles, throw in the sliced onions and fry to a light brown; remove and set aside. Then put in half a pound, or a coonkee, of the best bassmuttee or cheeneesuckur, having drained away all the water in which it was washed, and fry. On the rice absorbing the ghee, throw in a few cloves, four or five cardamoms, half a dozen small sticks of cinnamon, some peppercorns, a blade or two of mace, and one dessert-spoonful of salt. Mix up the whole, and pour over it the gravy in which the chicken and beef were boiled, or as much of it only as will entirely cover the rice; close the pot immediately with a close-fitting cover, and set on a slow fire. As the gravy continues to decrease or to be absorbed, so keep reducing the fire, shaking up the pot occasionally, or stirring its contents, to prevent the pellow from burning. Brown the boiled chicken in a pan with ghee or butter, and serve up as follows:—

Place the chicken, either whole or cut up, on the centre of a dish, covering it with the pellow; strew over it the fried onions, garnishing it besides with two hard-boiled eggs, cut into halves, or in some device, and with half a dozen bits of finely-sliced and fried bacon, to suit the taste of those who like the latter.

13.—Beef, Mutton, or Kid Pellow.

Take two pounds of beef, and cut up as for a curry, or take a small but good leg of mutton, or two legs of a kid, rejecting the loin.

Make a good, strong gravy with seasoning of sliced onions, ginger, and salt, with water, which when cooked down will be reduced to about sufficient only to cover the rice. Then proceed to make the pellow in all respects as directed in the foregoing recipe. The beef is not further used for the table, but treat the legs of the kid, or the mutton, the same as the chicken, and serve up with fried onions, hard-boiled eggs, and fried bacon, like the chicken pellow.

14.—Prawn Pellow.

Instead of a chicken, provide yourself with eight or ten good-sized "bagda prawns," and a good hard cocoanut. After frying and setting aside the sliced onions, as directed above, the rice is to be fried, but, instead of using chicken or any other meat broth, cook it in the milk of the cocoanut (*vide* recipe No. 54), observing in all particulars the instructions given for the chicken pellow, recipe No. 12, and serve up as follows:—Dish up the pellow, strew over it the fried onions, and garnish with the prawns finely boiled, and two hard-boiled eggs cut in halves or in some device.

The cocoanut milk will impart a sweetish flavour to the pellow, but it is not disagreeable; and its sweetness may be subdued, if required, by reducing the strength of the cocoanut milk.

15.—Lobster or Fish Pellow.

Take out the centre bones of one or two hilsa or beckty fishes, which are procurable fresh and good in the market, and eight or ten large long-legged lobsters with the roe or coral; thoroughly wash in several waters with salt, and boil with plenty of seasoning of onions, sliced ginger, peppercorns, a dozen bay-leaves, a tablespoonful of unroasted dhuniah or coriander seed, and salt, with water sufficient to give the required quantity of gravy. When ready, remove and shell the lobsters, reserving the roe or red coral in the heads, which bruise down with a little unroasted coriander seed, and mix with the fish gravy. Make the pellow in all other respects the same as prawn pellow, using the gravy of the fish instead of cocoanut or other gravy, and garnish with the lobsters, &c.

CURRIES.

A CURRY-STONE and muller, or what the natives call ***seal our lurriah***, are necessary for the preparation of condiments for daily use. The condiments should be carefully, and each kind separately, ground down to a nice paste with a little water.

Condiments prepared with water will not keep good any number of days; if required for a journey, therefore, or as presents for friends at home, good sweet oil and the best English vinegar should be substituted for the water. For the preparation of condiments for this purpose see recipe No. 65.

The first cost of a curry-stone and muller of large size will not exceed one rupee, but they will require re-cutting every three or four months, at a cost not exceeding one anna each re-setting.

The following is a list of curry condiments and hotspice in almost daily use:—

Curry onions, or *carree ka piaj*,	price from	3 to 8 pice	per seer.
Turmeric, or *huldee*	,,	3 to 5 annas	,,
Garlic, or *lussoon*	,,	2 to 3 annas	,,
Green ginger, or *uddruck*	,,	2 to 4 annas	,,
Dry chilies, or *sooka mirritch*	,,	3 to 5 annas	,,
Coriander-seed, or *dhunnia*	,,	3 to 4 annas	,,
Cumin-seed, or *jeerah*	,,	5 to 6 annas	,,
Peppercorns, or *gool mirritch*	,,	5 to 6 annas	,,
Bay-leaves, or *tage paththa*	,,	2 to 3 annas	,,
Lemon-grass, or *uggheaghass*	,,	2 to 6 pice for a bundle of 16 to 20 blades of grass.	
Poppy-seed, or *post ka danna*	,,	3 to 4 annas per seer.	
Onion-seed, or *cullinga*	,,	5 to 8 annas	,,
Stick cinnamon, or *dalcheenee*	Mixed; prices range from Rs. 3-14 to 4 per seer.		
Cardamoms, or *elachee*			
Cloves, or *loung*			
Nutmeg, or *jyephall*			
Mace, or *jowitree*			

However high prices may range, one rupee-worth of mixed condiments, including hotspice, will suffice for a month's consumption for a party of from four to six adults, allowing for three curries per day, cutlets and made dishes included.

GRAVY CURRIES.

The following directions for an every-day gravy chicken curry will apply equally to all ordinary meat gravy curries:—

16.—Chicken Curry.

Take one chittack or two ounces of ghee, two breakfast-cupfuls of water, one teaspoonful and a half of salt, four teaspoonfuls of ground onions, one teaspoonful each of ground turmeric and chilies, half a teaspoonful of ground ginger, and a quarter of a teaspoonful of ground garlic.

To suit the taste of those who like it, half a teaspoonful of ground coriander-seed may be added, which should be roasted before being ground. Observe the following directions for cooking:—

Take the usual full-sized curry chicken, the price of which has latterly ranged from three to four annas, and divide it into sixteen or eighteen pieces. Warm the pot, melt in it the ghee, and immediately it begins to bubble throw in all the ground condiments, stirring until quite brown; then put in the cut-up chicken and the salt, and stir up to a good light-brown colour; then add the water, and allow the whole to simmer over a slow fire until the chicken is quite tender, and the liquid reduced to about half its original quantity. The operation of cooking or simmering will take from a half to three-quarters of an hour.

17.—Kid Curry.

Take a hind-quarter or a fore-quarter of kid, which may be obtained at from three to four annas the quarter; cut it up into sixteen or eighteen pieces; take condiments in the proportion given in recipe No. 16, and cook it in every particular the same as the chicken curry, allowing it to simmer three-quarters of an hour.

18.—Veal Curry.

A small shoulder of veal, the price of which ranges from three to four annas, may be selected; cut off from it sixteen or eighteen one-inch square pieces of the best part of the meat, and curry it in every particular the same as a chicken, only allowing it to simmer half to three-quarters of an hour.

19.—Mutton Curry.

Obtain a small shoulder at from five to six annas; cut it up into sixteen or eighteen one-inch square pieces, rejecting all the bones; curry it the same as a chicken, allowing it to simmer for half an hour longer, or until the meat is tender.

N.B.—The bones of the veal and mutton, referred to in this and the foregoing recipe, may be turned to account for stock or gravy for some made dish.

20.—Beef Curry.

Two pounds of well-selected meat will cost from three to four annas; cut it up into one-inch square pieces, rejecting all the scraggy parts;

cook it in every respect according to the instructions given in recipe No. 16 for cooking a gravy chicken curry, only allowing it to simmer for a much longer time than any other curry, or until the beef becomes tender.

21.—Green Duck Curry.

The price of a young tender duck may be quoted at from four to five annas. Cut it up exactly as you would a chicken, and curry it in the same manner, allowing it to simmer for an hour and a half. It is desirable to introduce half a teaspoonful each of coriander and cumin seeds in this curry.

22.—Young Pigeon Curry.

Take four young pigeons; cut each into four pieces, making in all sixteen pieces. The price of young pigeons ranges from five to six annas the pair. The instructions given for the cooking of a gravy chicken curry apply equally to a pigeon curry.

DOOPIAJAS.

THE literal translation of *doopiaja* is "two onions," and the term probably is correctly applicable, as it will be noticed, in the recipes for preparing the *doopiaja curries*, that besides the full quantity of ground onions, it is necessary to put in about an equal quantity of fried onions, thereby *doubling* the quantity of onions.

Doopiajas are more piquant curries; they are cooked with more ghee and less water. The following condiments, &c., are considered ample for a really good *doopiaja* of chicken or of any meat:—

One chittack and a half or three ounces of ghee, one breakfast-cupful of water, one teaspoonful and a half of salt, four teaspoonfuls of ground onions, one teaspoonful each of ground turmeric and chilies, half a teaspoonful of ground ginger, a quarter of a teaspoonful of ground garlic, twelve onions cut lengthways, each into six or eight slices, and half a teaspoonful of ground coriander-seed if it be liked.

23.—Chicken Doopiaja.

Take a full-sized curry chicken and divide it into sixteen or eighteen pieces. Melt the ghee in a warm or heated pot, fry brown the sliced onions and set aside; then fry the ground condiments, stirring the whole; when brown, add the cut-up chicken with the salt, and fry to a rich brown. Chop the fried onions and put into the pot with one cup of water, and allow to simmer over a slow fire for about one hour, when the chicken will be perfectly tender, and the liquid reduced to a thick consistency, and to half its original quantity.

24.—Kid Doopiaja

Is made in all respects as a chicken doopiaja, the kid to be cut up in the usual manner. The hind quarter is preferable to the fore quarter.

25.—Veal Doopiaja.

Take only the meat from a shoulder, cut it up into squares, and allow it to simmer for half an hour longer than the chicken doopiaja.

26.—Mutton Doopiaja.

The flesh part of a shoulder is cut up in squares and doopiajed exactly as a chicken, allowing it to simmer over a slow fire for half an hour longer.

27.—Beef Doopiaja.

Cut two pounds of beef into one-inch square pieces, and follow all the instructions given in recipe No. 23, only allowing it to simmer for a much longer time over a slow fire, until the beef is perfectly tender.

28.—Duck Doopiaja.

Divide as you would a chicken, and cook the duck in the same manner, allowing it to simmer a little longer than the chicken doopiaja. Half a teaspoonful each of ground coriander and cumin seed should be mixed with the condiments.

29.—Doopiaja of Pigeons.

Take four pigeons, cut each into four pieces, and proceed in every particular the same as for a chicken doopiaja.

30.—Cold Boiled Pork Doopiaja.

Cut from the remains of cold boiled pork sixteen one-inch square pieces, and doopiaje it in the way directed for a chicken. The time required to simmer will not exceed that allowed for the chicken doopiaja.

31.—Udder Doopiaja.

Take two pounds of udder; before cutting it into squares, it should be parboiled, and then made into doopiaja, allowing it to simmer over a slow fire for about two hours.

32.—Udder and Beef Doopiaja.

Take one pound each of udder and beef; parboil the udder, and then cut it up with the beef into one-inch square pieces, and doopiaje it, allowing it to simmer for about two hours.

It is necessary to impress on the amateur artist the importance of paying particular attention to the firing: a brisk fire will dry up the ghee and the water before the curry is half cooked, and necessitate the addition of more water, which will in every instance spoil the doopiaja, although the addition of a little water, if such be necessary when the curry is nearly cooked, will do it no harm. In every instance where ghee, butter, &c., is to be melted, it is desirable first to warm the pot.

FORCEMEAT BALL CURRIES, OR COFTA-KA-CARREE.

Beef, mutton, chicken, fish, crabs, and prawns are usually taken for making these curries. The ingredients for two pounds of meat or fish are as follow:—Lard, ghee, or mustard oil, three to four ounces; water or stock, five to six ounces; ground onions, one tablespoonful or one ounce; ground chilies, a quarter of a tablespoonful; ground turmeric, a quarter of a tablespoonful; ground green ginger, half a teaspoonful; ground peppercorns, half a teaspoonful; ground garlic, a quarter of a teaspoonful; garden herbs, finely chopped, one dessertspoonful; salt, one dessertspoonful; finely-grated bread-crumbs, three tablespoonfuls; one egg.

N.B.—In the fish, crab, and prawn coftas the ginger must be omitted.

33.—Beef Forcemeat Ball Curry.

Get rather more than two pounds of good fat beef; wash it thoroughly, and cut it into pieces, rejecting all veins and scraggy portions; put about two pounds of it into a mortar and pound it fine, removing all fibres, veins, &c., and if it be desired put up a broth of all the rejections. Mix with the pounded beef a teaspoonful of salt, pepper, and garden herbs, and two tablespoonfuls of bread-crumbs; add a little of the broth, or in its absence some milk; mix the whole well together; beat up the yolk and white of the egg, add it to the mixture, and make into balls about the size of large walnuts; roll them in bread-crumbs. After heating the pot, melt the lard or ghee, and fry brown the ground ingredients, sprinkling a tablespoonful of cold water over them; then add the coftas or balls with salt to taste, and fry or brown them; after which pour into the pot either a cup of broth or of water, and allow to simmer for about two hours.

N.B.—Some cooks add to the beef cofta curries ground hot spices, which are fried with the curry condiments, and are suited to most tastes.

34.—Chicken Forcemeat Ball Curry.

Procure a good fat chicken and a quarter of a pound of beef suet; put the suet into a mortar with all the fleshy parts of the chicken, and pound to a pulp; make a stock of gravy of the bones; mix with the pounded meat all the several ingredients named in the foregoing recipe, with the addition of an egg well beaten up; make into balls, roll in bread-crumbs, and curry as directed above.

N.B.—The chicken cofta curry may also be made without any suet; the general practice is to get chickens rather larger than those usually selected for ordinary curries.

35.—Mutton Forcemeat Ball Curry.

Take the best parts of a leg or shoulder of mutton; cut them up, wash, and pound well down; make a gravy of the bones and rejections; mix with the pounded mutton all the ingredients mentioned in the recipe for making beef balls, and cook exactly as the beef cofta curry.

36.—Ball Curry of Liver and Udder.

Get one pound each of liver and udder; thoroughly wash and parboil them, then cut them into pieces, put into a mortar, and pound them to a pulp; mix with pepper, salt, herbs, bread-crumbs, and an egg; make into balls, and curry them in the same manner as any of the foregoing forcemeat ball curries.

37.—Prawn Cofta Curry.

Get thirty to forty of the best prawns, and remove the heads and shells; wash the prawns well with salt and water, then pound them to a pulp; mix with it all the ingredients as directed for the beef cofta; make into balls, roll them in bread-crumbs, and set aside. After washing the heads, remove the shells, and bruise the contents with a dessertspoonful of unroasted coriander-seed; take all the juice, and fry it with the ground condiments; then put in the balls, brown them, add salt to taste, a cup of water, and simmer until they are cooked.

N.B.—Good mustard oil is preferable to using lard or ghee, and the ginger must be omitted; but the addition of a few bay-leaves and blades of lemon-grass would be an improvement. It is not usual to dish up the lemon-grass.

38.—Lobster Cofta Curry.

According to their size, take eight or ten lobsters; clean them thoroughly; remove the heads and shells; pull the flesh to pieces and pound to a pulp; add to it some of the red coral from the head, then mix into it the bread-crumbs, salt, pepper, herbs, and an egg well beaten up, and make into balls. The remains of the heads and the contents of the long legs bruise down with unroasted coriander-seed; take all the juice and fry it in mustard oil with the ground condiments omitting the ginger, and cook the balls in the same way as the prawn balls, with the addition of bay-leaves and a few blades of lemon-grass. Lemon-grass is not served up.

39.—Crab Cofta Curry.

Select ten or twelve *gheewalla kakarahs*, or crabs full of the red coral; wash them thoroughly, then boil them; remove all the meat and coral out of the shells, pound to a pulp, and, after mixing all the ingredients and fixing them with an egg well beaten up, make into balls, and cook them in all respects according to the directions for lobster cofta curry. Time to simmer: say half an hour.

40.—Fish Cofta Curry.

Cold boiled or fried fish is the best adapted for making coftas; it not necessary to give other instructions than those already given at length in the foregoing recipes, excepting that mustard oil is the best adapted for fresh-fish curries.

N.B.—The remains of hermetically-sealed fish, such as salmon and mackerel, removed from dinner, are well adapted for making cofta curries.

Under-done roast meats, such as beef, mutton, veal, and fowl, will make excellent cofta curries.

COUNTRY CAPTAIN.

The country captain is usually made of chicken, and occasionally of kid and veal. Cold meats and curries are also sometimes converted into this dish, the condiments for which are as follow:—Two chittacks or four ounces of ghee, half a teaspoonful of ground chilies, one teaspoonful of salt, a quarter of a teaspoonful of ground turmeric, and twenty onions, cut up lengthways into fine slices.

41.—Chicken Country Captain.

Cut up in the usual way an ordinary curry chicken. Warm the ghee and fry the sliced onions, which when brown set aside; fry the ground turmeric and chilies, then throw in the chicken and salt, and continue to fry, stirring the whole, until the chicken is tender. Serve it up, strewing over it the fried onions.

42.—Kid Country Captain.

Before cutting up the kid, a four-quarter, let it be partially broiled or roasted, and then make it into country captain in accordance with the above directions; or, instead of partially roasting the kid, add half a cup of water to assist the meat to dissolve.

43.—Veal Country Captain.

Partially broil or roast a shoulder of veal before cutting it up; or make the country captain as directed in recipe No. 42, by adding half a cup of water instead of partially broiling the meat.

44.—Jhal Frezee.

Cut up into small squares, of less than an inch, either cold mutton, beef, or veal, rejecting the bones; add a large quantity of sliced onions some chilies cut up, and a teaspoonful of salt. Warm a chittack, or two ounces of ghee, and throw into it the meat, onions, chilies, and salt, and allow to simmer, or fry, stirring the whole while, until the onions are quite tender.

HINDOOSTANEE CURRIES.

45.—Seik Kawab

Is usually eaten with chappatee or hand-bread, and only occasionally with rice, and contains the following condiments:—Two tablespoonfuls of mustard oil, four teaspoonfuls of ground onions, one teaspoonful of ground chilies, half a teaspoonful of ground ginger, a quarter of a teaspoonful of ground garlic, one teaspoonful of ground turmeric, one teaspoonful and a half of salt, a cup of thick tyre or dhye, half a teaspoonful of ground coriander-seed, the juice of one large lemon, and a little ghee.

Take two pounds of beef, mutton, or veal; remove the bones, and chop the meat slightly, without mincing or cutting through it; mix well together all the ground condiments, including the oil, tyre, and lemon-juice, in which steep the chopped meat, turning it over occasionally to absorb the mixture. After a while cut up the meat into squares of equal size, say two inches, and continue to keep them in the mixture for fully one hour; then pass the squares of meat either on a silver, plated, or other metal skewer, and roast or broil over a slow charcoal fire, basting the whole time with ghee, to allow the kawab to become of a rich brown colour, without burning or being singed in the basting. Remove from the skewer, and serve hot.

46.—Tick-keeah Kawab.

Take two pounds of fat beef, wash it, cut it into small pieces, and pound it to a pulp, remove all fibres, &c., and then add to it one teaspoonful of ground onion, a quarter of a teaspoonful of ground turmeric, one-eighth of a teaspoonful of ground garlic, a quarter of a teaspoonful of ground chilies, half a teaspoonful of ground peppercorns, a quarter of a teaspoonful of ground ginger, half a teaspoonful of ground hot spices, and one tablespoonful of tyre or dhye.

Mix the whole well together, add salt to your taste, and the yolk and white of an egg well beaten up; form into balls of equal sizes; flatten them, pass them on iron or plated skewers about eighteen inches long, rub them well over with ghee, wrap them in plantain-leaf, and roast or broil them over a charcoal fire. Serve them up hot, removed from the skewers. These are usually eaten with chappatee.

HUSSANEE CURRIES, OR CURRIES ON STICK.

THE ingredients and condiments necessary for the curries on stick are as follow:—One chittack and a half of ghee, one teaspoonful and a half of salt, four teaspoonfuls of ground onions, one teaspoonful of turmeric, half a teaspoonful of ginger, half a cupful of water, a quarter of a teaspoonful of ground garlic, one teaspoonful of chilies, half a cupful of tyre or dhye, some finely-sliced ginger, and as many small curry onions cut into half as may be required. Six silver pins five inches long or, in the absence of these, six bamboo pins, are required.

47.—Hussanee Beef Curry.

Cut up two pounds of beef into small squares not exceeding one inch, and pass them on the silver or bamboo pins alternately with half an onion and a slice of ginger. Half a dozen sticks will be ample for four hearty consumers.

Warm the ghee and brown the ground condiments; then put in the sticks of meat, and brown, stirring the whole; after this add the tyre and a little water, and allow to simmer over a slow fire for nearly two hours, when the curry will be ready. Serve up on a curry-dish without removing the sticks.

48.—Hussanee Mutton Curry.

Remove the meat from a shoulder of mutton, and cut it into small squares; the same instructions will apply to the preparation of mutton curry on stick as those given for beef curry on stick. Time to simmer: half an hour.

49.—Hussanee Veal Curry.

Cut squares enough from a shoulder of veal, and observe the instructions given in the foregoing recipe. Time to simmer: one hour.

50.—Hussanee Curry of Udder and Liver.

The udder and liver should be parboiled before being cut up for passing on the sticks; but in all other respects the instructions given for the beef and mutton curries on stick will apply to the udder and liver curry on stick. Time to simmer: fully one hour and a half.

KURMA OR QUOREMA CURRY.

This, without exception, is one of the richest of Hindoostanee curries, but it is quite unsuited to European taste, if made according to the original recipe, of which the following is a copy:—

51.—Quorema Curry, Plain.

Take two pounds of mutton, one pound of tyre or dhye, two chittacks of garlic, one dam of cardamoms, four chittacks of bruised almonds, four mashas of saffron, the juice of five lemons, one pound of ghee, four chittacks of sliced onions, one dam of cloves, one chittack of pepper, four chittacks of cream, and a quarter of a teaspoonful of ground garlic.

The following is the recipe of the quorema curry usually put on a gentleman's table:—Two chittacks and a half or five ounces of ghee, one cup or eight ounces of good thick tyre, one teaspoonful of ground chilies, four teaspoonfuls of ground onions, one teaspoonful of coriander-seed, six small sticks of ground cinnamon, two or three blades of lemon-grass, one teaspoonful and a half of salt, a half teaspoonful of ground ginger, a quarter of a teaspoonful of ground garlic, eight or ten peppercorns, four or five ground cloves, five or six ground cardamoms, two or three bay-leaves, a quarter of a cup of water, the juice of one lemon, and twelve large onions cut lengthways into fine slices.

Take two pounds of good fat mutton, and cut it up into pieces nearly one inch and a half square. Warm the ghee, fry in it the sliced onions, and set aside; then fry all the ground condiments, including the ground hot spices. When quite brown, throw in the mutton and salt, and allow the whole to brown, after which add the tyre, the hot spices with peppercorns and bay-leaves, the lemon-grass, the water, and the fried onions finely chopped; close the pot, and allow it to simmer over a gentle coal fire for about an hour and a half or two hours, by which time the kurma will be quite ready. The blades of lemon-grass are never dished up.

52.—Kid Quorema.

Cut up a fore-quarter or a hind-quarter of a kid into eight or ten pieces, and cook it exactly as directed in the foregoing recipe. This is rather preferred to mutton quorema.

53.—Fowl Quorema.

Take a young full-grown tender fowl; cut it up as for an ordinary curry, cook it with all the condiments in the proportions given, and observe all the directions laid down in recipe No. 51.

N.B.—Most Europeans give the preference to the fowl quorema.

MALAY CURRIES.

THE condiments and other ingredients necessary are as follow:—One chittack or two ounces of ghee, one teaspoonful and a half of salt, four teaspoonfuls of ground onions, one teaspoonful of ground turmeric, one teaspoonful of ground chilies, half a teaspoonful of ground ginger, a quarter of a teaspoonful of ground garlic, the milk of a large cocoanut, say two cups, two blades of lemon-grass, three or four cloves, ground, three or four cardamoms, and as many small sticks of cinnamon, ground.

The coriander and cumin seeds must on no account be put into malay curries, or the delicate flavour of the cocoanut will be destroyed.

It will be necessary to provide what the natives call a *narial-ka-khoornee*, which, interpreted, means "cocoanut scraper." It is a small circular flat piece of iron, about the size and thickness of a Spanish dollar, the edges being notched. It is of rude construction, and fixed on a conveniently-shaped wooden frame, also of rude construction. The best of the kind may be procured for two annas.

54.—Cocoanut Milk.

The nut is scraped or rasped with the aid of the "khoornee" into very fine particles; it is then put into a deep vessel, and boiling water poured over it until the whole of the scraped cocoanut is covered. After allowing it to steep for ten or fifteen minutes, it is carefully strained through a clean napkin into another vessel or cup, the pulp is returned into the original vessel, and more boiling water is poured over it. This operation of steeping in boiling water and straining is continued until you have obtained the required quantity of the extracted milk of the cocoanut. The pulp is thrown away. If the cocoanut be a small one, or its nut not hard and deep, it will be necessary to provide a second cocoanut. Good cocoanuts are sold at an anna to an anna and a half a piece.

55.—Chicken Malay Gravy Curry with White Pumpkin or Cucumber.

Take the usual full-sized curry chicken, and divide it as before directed; get either six cucumbers or a quarter of a white pumpkin; remove the green skin and the part containing the seeds, then cut it up into sixteen pieces of about two inches square, and steep in water.

Fry in the ghee all the ground condiments, including the ground hot spices; when brown, add the cut-up chicken and salt; fry to a fine bright light brown; then put in the pumpkin, having previously allowed all the water to drain away through a colander; pour in the two cups of cocoanut milk, the lemon-grass, and hot spices, and allow the whole to simmer over a slow fire for about half an hour, when the curry will be ready: the blade of lemon-grass is not dished up.

56.—Prawn Malay Gravy Curry with White Pumpkin or Cucumber.

Select the bagda prawns (*bagda chingree*), whenever they are procurable, in preference to any other description. The shell and head are of a dark colour in comparison with what are called *jeel ka chingree*, the shell and head of which are very perceptibly several shades lighter than the *bagdas*.

It is impossible to quote any price as a guide, the fluctuation being almost incredible. Fine large prawns, not lobsters—prawns which, without their heads, would be about the size of the ordinary dried Normandy pippins sent out to this country for tarts—may be obtained one day at two annas for twenty, and the next day they will not be procurable at less than eight annas for the same number. This remark applies generally to fish of every description brought for sale into the Calcutta market.

With one other remark of importance, we shall proceed to the instructions necessary for the preparation of the prawn malay gravy curry.

The prawns should be parboiled after removing the heads, to rid them, as the natives call it, of *besine*, which means all disagreeable character of fishy smell and taste.

As a rule, the heads of prawns should always be rejected, which, in the process of frying, absorb largely the ghee, and in the cooking dispel a liquid from their spongy formation.

In all other respects, the prawn gravy malay curry is cooked like the chicken malay gravy curry, omitting the ginger; but an additional blade or two of the lemon-grass would not be amiss, which, on the curry being dished, are thrown away.

57.—Chicken Malay Gravy Curry with Pulwal.

Take a fat chicken, clean it, remove all the flesh and pound it to a pulp, and prepare it in every respect as directed in recipe No. 34 for a cofta curry, omitting the suet. Take a dozen large-sized pulwals, scrape or pare away the outer skin, split them down one side, extract all the seeds, &c., and throw the pulwals into cold water; wash and drain away all the water, then stuff them with the prepared forcemeat, tie them with fine sewing cotton, and cook them in the milk of cocoanut, exactly as directed in recipe No. 55.

58.—Prawn Malay Gravy Curry with Pulwal.

Take bagda prawns; shell and clean them, pound to a pulp, and prepare as directed in recipe No. 37 for prawn cofta curry. Take a dozen pulwals, peel them finely, cut them open lengthways, clear them of all seeds, &c., wash and dry them, then stuff them with the prepared prawn mince; tie the pulwals with sewing cotton, and cook in cocoanut milk as directed in recipe No. 56.

59.—Chicken Malay Doopiaja.

The condiments and ingredients are as follow:—One chittack and a half or three ounces of ghee, one teaspoonful and a half of salt, four teaspoonfuls of ground onions, one teaspoonful of ground turmeric, one teaspoonful of ground chilies, half a teaspoonful of ground ginger, a quarter of a teaspoonful of ground garlic, one cup of strong cocoanut milk, and one dozen onions cut lengthways into fine slices.

Cut up the chicken in the usual manner, warm the ghee, fry and set aside the sliced onions, then fry brown the ground condiments, after which add the chicken and salt. When fried brown, pour in the cocoanut milk and the fried onions finely chopped, and allow to simmer over a slow fire: the Malay doopiaja will be ready in an hour.

60.—Prawn Malay Doopiaja.

Take sixteen or twenty large bagda prawns, throw away the heads, parboil the prawns, and then doopiaje in all respects as for a chicken Malay doopiaja, omitting the ginger.

PORTUGUESE CURRY (VINDALOO OR BINDALOO).

THIS well-known Portuguese curry can only be made properly of beef, pork, or duck. The following is a recipe of the vindaloo in general use:—

Six ounces or three chittacks of ghee or lard, one tablespoonful of bruised garlic, one tablespoonful of ground garlic, one tablespoonful of ground ginger, two teaspoonfuls of ground chilies, one teaspoonful of roasted and ground coriander-seed, half a teaspoonful of roasted and ground cumin-seed, two or three bay-leaves, a few peppercorns, four or five cloves, roasted and ground, four or five cardamoms, roasted and ground, six small sticks of cinnamon, roasted and ground, with half a cup of good vinegar, to two pounds of pork or beef or a duck.

N.B.—The best vindaloo is that prepared with mustard oil.

61.—Beef Vindaloo.

Cut up two pounds of fat beef into large squares, and steep them in the vinegar, together with half a teaspoonful of salt and all the ground condiments, from eighteen to twenty-four hours. Then warm the ghee or lard and throw in the meat, together with the condiments and vinegar in which it had been steeped, adding a few peppercorns and bay-leaves, and allow to simmer gently over a slow fire for two hours, or until the meat is perfectly tender, and serve up hot.

62.—Pork Vindaloo.

Cut up two pounds of fat pork into large squares, and curry according to the directions given in the foregoing recipe, omitting the cloves, cardamoms, and cinnamon.

63.—Duck Vindaloo.

Take a young, full-grown, but tender duck; cut it up as for a curry, and put it through the same course of pickling from eighteen to twenty-four hours before being cooked.

64.—Pickled Vindaloo (adapted as a Present to Friends at a Distance).

If the following instructions be carried out carefully, the vindaloo will keep good for months, and, if required, may be sent as an acceptable present to friends at home.

In order to keep it good sufficiently long to be sent home round the Cape, select the fattest parts of pork; satisfy yourself that the meat is fresh and sound, and that it has not been washed with water in the butcher's shop. Cut the meat into two-inch squares, wash thoroughly in vinegar (no water), rub over with the following condiments, and then steep them in really good English vinegar for twenty-four hours:—Garlic bruised, not ground down, dry ginger powdered, turmeric powdered, peppercorns roasted and powdered, coriander-seeds roasted and powdered, cumin-seeds roasted and powdered, and dry salt.

Melt a large quantity of the best mustard oil in an earthen pot, and, according to the quantity of meat, take additional condiments mentioned above, but in the proportion given in recipe No. 61; grind in vinegar, and fry in the oil; then put in the meat, and all the vinegar, &c., in which it had been steeped, together with some more salt, a little more vinegar, a few bay-leaves and peppercorns, and allow to simmer until the meat is quite tender. Remove from the fire and allow it to get quite cold; then put it into dry stone jars, with patent screw tops, well filled with plenty of the oil in which the vindaloo was cooked. Take care that all the meat is well covered over with oil, which latter ought to be at least from two to three inches above the meat in the jar. Screw down the lid, and cover it over with a good sound bladder to render it perfectly air-tight.

When required for use, take out only as much as will suffice, and simply warm it in a little of its own gravy.

65.—Curry Paste

Is likewise adapted for sending as a present to friends at home. It is made in the following manner:—Eight ounces of dhunnia, or coriander-seed, roasted; one ounce of jeerah, or cumin-seed, roasted; two ounces of huldee, or dry turmeric; two ounces of lal mirritch, dry chilies; two ounces of kala mirritch, black pepper, roasted; two ounces of rai, or mustard-seed; one ounce of soat, or dry ginger; one ounce of lussan, or garlic; four ounces of nimmuck, salt; four ounces of cheenee, or sugar; four ounces of chunna or gram dal without husk, and roasted. The above ingredients, in the proportions given, to be carefully pounded and ground down with the best English white wine vinegar to the consistency of a thick jelly; then warm some good sweet oil, and while bubbling fry in it the mixture until it is reduced to a paste; let it cool, and then bottle it.

N.B.—Great care must be taken not to use any water in the preparation, and mustard oil is better adapted than sweet oil for frying the mixture in.

MADRAS MULLIGATAWNY CURRY.

As this dish is usually served up and partaken of in the place of ordinary soup, reference will be made to it hereafter under the head of "Soups."

Before proceeding to remark on fish, vegetable, and peas curries, a few useful hints and suggestions may be offered on meat curries generally.

In many families the remains of cold meat, if not required for other purposes, are made into curry: cold roast or boiled mutton is admirably adapted for the purpose; and in ninety-nine cases out of a hundred consumers cannot tell the difference. If there be any difference or advantage, it is decidedly in favour of the cold meat: the roasting joints are always of a superior quality to meats sold under the designation of "curry meats."

The remains of cold roast beef make the best cofta curries, croquets, &c., and if the beef be under-done no fresh beef will make a better doopiaja.

Vegetables are sometimes put into gravy meat curries, never into doopiajas; but, as a rule, the introduction of vegetable into any meat curry is objectionable, from the fact that all vegetables in the process of boiling or cooking throw out a liquid, some more and some less: the potato throws out the least, but of a disagreeable character. It is true potatoes may be boiled before being put into a curry, but the piquancy and peculiarity of flavour looked for in a curry is so palpably destroyed that the innovation may be discovered with closed eyes. The introduction of vegetable into gravy fish curries, however, is no innovation, as the condiments used for the one answer for the other; both are cooked in oil, and the ginger omitted.

66.—GRAVY FISH CURRIES.

The condiments are as follow:—Mustard oil, one chittack or two ounces; water, two cups; four teaspoonfuls of ground onions, one teaspoonful of ground turmeric, one teaspoonful of ground chilies, and a quarter of a teaspoonful of garlic.

It will be noticed that mustard oil is used instead of ghee, and no ginger.

Too much care cannot be observed in thoroughly cleaning, rubbing, and washing the fish in salt and water before cooking it for the table. Fish, if properly washed, when served up will never be offensive, unless it be bad when purchased.

67.—Hilsa Fish Gravy Curry.

The head and tail are thrown away, and the fish cut into slices of rather more than half an inch thick; these should be washed in several waters with salt, to rid them of all "besine," before they are curried.

The acid of tamarind is considered an improvement, or "amchoor," which is sliced green mangoe dried in salt.

68.—Beckty Fish Gravy Curry

Is sliced and washed in salt like the hilsa before being cooked. It is not usual to put any acid in the beckty fish curry.

69.—Prawn Doopiaja.

Take one chittack and a half of mustard oil, four teaspoonfuls of ground onions, one teaspoonful of ground turmeric, one teaspoonful of ground chilies, a quarter of a teaspoonful of garlic, twelve curry onions cut lengthways, each into six or eight slices, one cupful of water, and twelve large prawns.

Clean and thoroughly wash the prawns, rejecting the heads, or taking only their substance pounded and squeezed out with unroasted coriander-seed, and after parboiling the prawns make the doopiaja in all respects according to the ordinary mode.

70.—Sliced Hilsa Fish Fried in Curry Condiments.

Take two teaspoonfuls of ground onions, one teaspoonful of ground chilies, two teaspoonfuls of salt, half a teaspoonful of ground turmeric, a quarter of a teaspoonful of ground garlic, and one chittack of mustard oil.

After slicing a hilsa in the manner directed for a curry, and having thoroughly cleaned and washed it with salt, rub into the slices all the ground condiments and the remaining salt, and allow them to remain for at least an hour. Warm the oil, and fry the slices of fish of a very light and bright brown. Serve up hot.

71.—Sliced Beckty Fish Fried in Curry Condiments.

Slice, wash, and fry exactly as directed above. Fish served up in this manner is well suited to some European tastes, and makes an agreeable change to the ordinary mode of frying fish for breakfast.

72.—EGG CURRY.

Take six or eight eggs, boil hard, shell, cut into halves, and set them aside; take ghee, ground condiments, and sliced fried onions, in all respects the same as for a chicken doopiaja, and observe precisely the same method of cooking, keeping in mind the fact that, the eggs being already cooked or boiled, a smaller quantity of water and a shorter time to simmer will suffice.

73.—Egg Curry with Green Peas.

This is a favourite curry with some families in winter, wl English green peas are procurable. The method of preparin exactly the same as recipe No. 71, allowing the curry to simm the peas are quite tender.

74.—Egg Curry, with Chunna Ka Dal.

Parboil the dal, say half a cupful; curry the dal first; whe nearly cooked, throw in the hard-boiled eggs, and finish the sin immediately the dal is soft or tender.

CHAHKEES.

CHAHKEE is a term applied to vegetable curries, some of wl deservedly popular, and one in particular, which many families ha during the season the vegetables are procurable, and yet never viz.—

75.—Seam, Potato, and Peas Chahkee.

Take twenty seams, four new potatoes, and a quarter of a seer peas; divide each seam into three pieces, and throw into a bowl o divide each potato into four pieces, and throw into water; shell t wash all thoroughly, put into a colander to drain, and cook w following condiments:—One chittack and a half of mustard oil, f spoonfuls of ground onions, one teaspoonful of ground chilies teaspoonful of ground turmeric, a quarter of a teaspoonful of garlic, one teaspoonful and a half of salt, and one cupful of water. the oil, let it bubble well, and fry the ground condiments; whe are quite brown put in the vegetables and salt; let the whole fry, it well; then add the water, and allow it to simmer over a slow f the vegetables are quite tender.

N.B.—A cauliflower may be added if required for a change.

76.—Pulwal, Potatoes, and Torrie.

Clean as much of the above three kinds of vegetables as will a vegetable-dish, and make the chahkee in all respects as the for

77.—Red Pumpkin and Tamarind.

A quarter of a red pumpkin and the pulp of two or three ta will be enough. Dissolve the pulp of the tamarind in the wa put it into the curry after the pumpkin has been fried.

78.—White Pumpkin and Tamarind.

Chahkee it in the same way as the red pumpkin.

79.—White Pumpkin, Plain, Cut Small.

It is not necessary to give any further instructions than those already given.

80.—Tomato with Tamarind.

Take twenty tomatoes and the pulp of two or three tamarinds, and chahkee as directed for red pumpkin.

81.—Tomato, Plain.

Chahkee twenty tomatoes according to instructions given for other chahkees.

N.B.—There is a fresh green herb called soa mattee, which is sometimes put into fish, vegetable, and other curries. Some Europeans like the flavour, and have it daily when procurable. Inquiry and trial are recommended.

SAUG CURRIES.

HALF an anna's worth of any saug will suffice for a party of four, for curries made of greens, such as spinach, &c. The following condiments, &c., are used:—One chittack and a half of mustard oil, four teaspoonfuls of ground onions, one teaspoonful of ground chilies, half a teaspoonful of ground turmeric, a quarter of a teaspoonful of ground garlic, one teaspoonful and a half of ground salt, and one cupful of water.

82.—Red Saug and Omra.

The omra should be peeled, and half fried if large. Great care must be taken to thoroughly clean and wash the greens. Put them into a colander and allow all the water to drain away. Then warm the oil, and fry the ground condiments; then the saug and omra, and when crisp add the water and cook over a slow fire until the greens and omra are tender.

83.—Red Saug, Omra, and Shrimps.

Observe in all respects the same process as that required in cooking without the shrimps, omitting the ginger.

84.—Red Saug and Prawns.

The prawns should be parboiled, and then follow all the instructions in recipe No. 82.

85.—Green Saug with Prawns.

Proceed in every particular as with the last.

86.—Danta Curry with Shrimps.

The danta is a fine delicate long green pod which the horseradish-tree yields, and contains small peas; these pods are cut into lengths of three or four inches and cooked with shrimps. Beyond this explanation it is not necessary to enlarge upon the instructions already given.

87.—Khuttah Carree, or Acid Vegetable Curry.

Take small quantities of all kinds of vegetables in season, but the best curry is that made of potatoes, kutchoo or artichoke, sweet potatoes or suckercund, carrots, red and white pumpkins, and tomatoes.

The vegetables should be cut into large pieces, and boiled in water with the following condiments:—Four teaspoonfuls of ground onions, one teaspoonful each of ground turmeric and chilies, a quarter of a teaspoonful of ground garlic, and one teaspoonful of roasted and ground coriander-seed.

Prepare two large cups of tamarind water, slightly sweetened with jaggry, strain through a sieve, and add the strained water to the boiled vegetables, with a few fresh chilies. Then melt in a separate pot one chittack or two ounces of mustard oil. While the oil is bubbling, fry in it a teaspoonful of the collinga, or onion-seeds, and when sufficiently fried pour it over the boiled vegetables including the tamarind water. Close up the pot, and allow it to simmer for fifteen to twenty minutes, when it will be ready. It is eaten cold.

BHAHJEES.

By *bhahjee* is meant fried. The two most generally approved vegetable bhahjees are those made of bringals and pulwals. The following are the condiments, &c., used:—Mustard oil according to the quantity of vegetable to be fried, a little ground turmeric and chilies, and some salt.

88.—Bringal Bhahjee.

Take young full-sized bringals; wash them thoroughly, and slice them about an eighth of an inch thick; dry them, steep them for half an hour in the ground condiments and salt, fry in oil, and serve up hot.

89.—Pulwal Bhahjee.

Take a dozen or more pulwals—a most excellent and wholesome native vegetable,—scrape or pare away very finely the upper green coating, divide them lengthways into two pieces, clear away all the seeds, &c., wash, drain away all the water, and steep them in ground turmeric, chilies, and salt for half an hour or longer; then fry them quite crisp in melted mustard oil. They are much liked by some Europeans.

N.B.—The vegetable called ram's horns or lady's fingers, known by the natives as *dharus*, makes an excellent bhahjee; so does the *kerrella*, a small green and intensely bitter native vegetable, which comes into the market in March and April; it is not, however, well suited to the European taste.

DAL OR PEAS CURRIES.

HALF an anna's worth of any dal will suffice for a party of four. The condiments are as follow:—Three-quarters of a chittack of ghee, four teaspoonfuls of ground onions, one teaspoonful of ground chilies, half a teaspoonful of ground turmeric, half a teaspoonful of ground ginger, a quarter of a teaspoonful of ground garlic, one teaspoonful and a half of salt, and half a dozen onions cut into six or eight slices each.

90.—Moong Dal.

Take half a pound of the raw dal, or say half a cupful; clean, pick, and roast it; mix it up with all the ground condiments and salt, put into a pot, pour water over the whole, some two inches above the dal, and boil it well, until the dal has quite dissolved. Be careful not to disturb it while in the process of boiling, but allow it to cake as it were *en masse*. When thoroughly boiled, churn the dal by twirling it in a wooden instrument called a *ghootnee;* then warm the ghee in a separate pot, fry the onions, chop them, and throw into the churned dal, after which pour the dal into the pot of melted ghee, and keep stirring until the dal and ghee have well mixed; then put the cover on, and allow to simmer over a slow fire for about a quarter of an hour.

N.B.—The standard price of the best roasted moong dal is two annas and a half per seer.

91.—Mussoor or Red Dal.

The process in all respects for preparing and cooking the red dal is the same as for the moong dal, excepting that, instead of fried sliced onions, a large clove of garlic is cut up small, fried, and takes the place of the onion.

The price of the best quality mussoor dal, free of husk, is two annas per seer.

92.—Mussoor Dal with Amchoor or with Tamarind.

Put the amchoor, or, if preferred, tamarind, into the pot with the dal; allow it to dissolve, and when the dal is going through the process of being churned remove the hard stones of the amchoor or seeds of the tamarind.

93.—Mussoor Dal Chur Churree.

Instead of only half a dozen onions, take a dozen, and cut them into fine slices lengthways. Warm the three-quarters of a chittack of ghee, fry and set aside the sliced onions, then fry all the ground condiments; next put in and fry the dal, having previously washed it well, soaked it in water for about a quarter of an hour, and drained it through a colander. When thoroughly fried and browned, add only a little water, barely sufficient to cover the fried dal, and allow to simmer from ten to fifteen minutes, or until the dal has dissolved. Serve up, strewing over it the fried onions. If chunna ka dal be used, soak it for an hour.

Other dals are occasionally served up, but very rarely at European tables. The price of the best clean chunna ka dal rarely exceeds two annas per seer.

94.—Dal Foolaree

Is much liked by Europeans, but is rarely served up well, owing to the trouble and time required in making it properly.

For the recipe see No. 223.

BURTAS OR MASHES.

BURTAS are mashes of potatoes and other vegetables, cold meats, dry fish, &c.; they are palatable, and much liked by most Europeans as accompaniments to curry and rice. The ingredients to almost every burta are the fine large white Patna onions, fresh green chilies, and the juice of fresh lemons.

95.—Potato Burta.

Take a moderate or middling sized white Patna onion; remove the outer coats, and slice very fine; then slice or cut up two hot green chilies, and squeeze over the onion and chilies the juice of a fresh lime: allow to soak. Take eight or ten well-boiled potatoes, half a teaspoonful of salt, and a teaspoonful of good mustard oil; bruise the potatoes down with a large silver or plated fork, adding, when they are half bruised, the onions and chilies, with as much only of the lime-juice as may be agreeable: mix all well together with a light hand, so that the potatoes may not cake, and yet be well and thoroughly mashed and mixed.

96.—Brinjal Burta.

Prepare the sliced onions, chilies, and lime-juice in the manner directed for potato burta. Take two fine young brinjals of large size; carefully and thoroughly roast them in a quick ash fire; remove the ashes and burnt parts of the skin, if any; then open the brinjals, and with a clean spoon remove the contents to as near the skin as possible, to which add a good teaspoonful of salt and a teaspoonful of mustard oil; work these with a spoon to a perfect pulp, throwing away the lumps or shreds if any; then mix with it all the onions, chilies, and lime-juice. If not to your taste, add more salt or lime-juice, according to fancy.

97.—Dry Fish Burta.

Prepare onions, chilies, and lime-juice as before. Take a part of the Arabian dried beckty and well broil it; remove all the bones, and pound the fish to nearly a powder; mix it thoroughly with a teaspoonful of mustard oil, and add the onions, chilies, and lime-juice.

98.—Red Herring Burta.

Take onions, chilies, and lime-juice. Place the herring, with its original paper packing, on a gridiron, or on a frying-pan, and warm it well; then clear it of all skin, very carefully pick out *all* the bones, bruise the herring, and mix it thoroughly with the sliced onions, chilies, and lime-juice.

N.B.—This is an inimitable burta.

99.—Cold Corned-Beef Burta.

Steep sliced onions and chilies in lime-juice; have the red well-corned part of a cold round of beef nicely pounded; add to it the onions, chilies, and as much of the lime-juice as may be desirable.

100.—Cold Tongue Burta.

The remains of a well-corned cold tongue make an excellent burta, as per recipe for cold beef burta.

101.—Cold Ham Burta

Is made in the same way as the beef and tongue burtas.

102.—Green Mango Burta.

The condiments for this burta are a quarter of a teaspoonful of ground chilies, half a teaspoonful of ground fresh mint-leaves, half a teaspoonful of ground ginger, half a teaspoonful of salt, and a teaspoonful of sugar.

Take two ordinary large-size green mangoes; peel, divide, and throw them into clean water, remove the stones, then bruise them to a perfect pulp with the aid of the curry-stone and muller. Care must be taken that the stone is perfectly clean, and will not impart the flavour of garlic or turmeric to the burta. Mix the sugar well with the pulp; if the mango be very acid, add a little more sugar; then mix it with the salt and ground condiments; more salt or sugar may be added if required.

103.—Tomato Burta.

Bake in an oven a dozen good-sized tomatoes until the skin cracks; break them down, and mix with them a little ground chilies, ginger, salt, and half a teaspoonful of good mustard oil. A small squeeze of lemon-juice may be added if desired.

SOUPS

A DIGESTER is best adapted for boiling soups in, as no steam can escape, and consequently less water is required than in a common pot.

To extract the substance or essence of meat, long and slow boiling over a charcoal fire is absolutely necessary. In the first instance, however, it is desirable to boil up the meat with pepper and salt on a quick, brisk fire, and take away all the black scum which rises to the surface; then pour a little cold water into the pot to raise up the white scum, which also remove, and reduce the fire, taking care that in the process of slow-boiling the pot is never off the boil.

104.—Shin of Beef Soup.

Take a shin of beef, cut it up small, wash it thoroughly, and boil with pepper and salt in sufficient water to well cover the meat. Let it boil over a brisk fire, taking away the black scum; add a little cold water, and skim off the white scum; then reduce the fire, and allow the soup to simmer until it somewhat thickens; strain the soup, cut away all the fat, season with soup herbs, and add more pepper and salt if necessary. Give it a good boil up, and then clear it with the white of an egg well beaten up, after which add a tablespoonful of Lea & Perrin's Worcestershire sauce, and half a wineglassful of sherry.

105.—Shin of Beef Soup, with Forcemeat and Egg Balls.

Prepare a shin of beef soup in all respects according to the above directions; clear with an egg well beaten up, add to it sauce, sherry, forcemeat, and egg balls.

106.—Vermicelli Soup.

Prepare a shin of beef soup as directed above, omitting the sauce and sherry. Parboil some vermicelli, and after clearing the soup with the white of an egg, add to it the parboiled vermicelli, and give it all a good boil up before serving.

107.—Macaroni Soup.

Prepare a shin of beef soup as directed above, omitting the sauce and wine; boil some macaroni until perfectly tender; clear the soup with the white of an egg, then add the boiled macaroni, and warm up before serving.

108.—Mulligatawny Soup.

Prepare a shin of beef soup as above, omitting the sauce, wine, and white of egg; set the soup aside. Take a full-sized curry chicken; cut it up into sixteen or eighteen pieces, and wash them thoroughly. Warm a pot and melt in it two chittacks or four ounces of ghee; fry in it some finely-sliced onions, and set aside. Then fry in the melted ghee the following condiments, &c.:—Four teaspoonfuls of ground onions, one teaspoonful of ground turmeric, one teaspoonful of ground chilies, half a teaspoonful of ground ginger, a quarter of a teaspoonful of ground garlic, half a teaspoonful of roasted and ground coriander-seed, and a quarter of a teaspoonful of roasted and ground cumin-seed.

Sprinkle a little water over these while frying; then add the cut-up chicken with two teaspoonfuls of salt. When nearly brown, add one chittack or two ounces of roasted and ground poppy-seeds; pour in the beef soup, add the fried onion and half a dozen of the *kurreeah fool* leaves, close the pot, and allow the whole to simmer over a slow fire until the chicken be perfectly tender. Serve up hot, with limes cut in slices on a separate plate.

109.—*Another Way.*

Prepare a shin of beef as directed above. Cut up a chicken; wash it and set it aside. Heat a pot and melt in it two chittacks or four ounces of ghee. After frying in it and setting aside some finely-sliced onions, fry the condiments in the proportions given in the foregoing recipe; then add the cut-up chicken with two teaspoonfuls of salt; brown it nicely; have ready two chittacks or four ounces of roasted and ground chunna ka or gram dal, which mix thoroughly in a cup of strong cocoanut milk, and pour over the chicken just as it has become brown; stir it well, and add the fried onions and the soup, with half a dozen of the *kurreeah fool* leaves; close the pot, and allow the whole to simmer for three-quarters of an hour. Serve up hot, with limes, either whole or cut in slices, on a separate plate.

110.—Delicious Curry Soup.

Prepare a strong beef soup; slice some onions, and cut up a chicken; take curry condiments as directed above, omitting the coriander and cumin seed; melt two chittacks or four ounces of ghee; fry and set aside the sliced onions, then fry the condiments, add the cut-up chicken, and fry that also. In a part of the beef soup boil a spoonful of tamarind, so as to separate the stocks and stones; strain and stir it into the fried chicken. After a while add the remainder of the beef soup, with half a dozen *kurreeah fool* leaves, and the fried onions; close up the pot, and continue to simmer the whole until the chicken is quite tender. Serve up hot.

111.—Bright Onion Soup.

Take a shoulder of veal; cut it up small, breaking all the bones; wash it thoroughly, put it into a pan with pepper, salt, and water, boil it well, and remove all the scum as it rises; reduce the fire, and let it simmer until the meat is perfectly dissolved; strain it, cut away all the fat, add soup herbs, and more pepper and salt if required; give it a boil up, and clear it with the white of an egg well beaten up; slice very fine some pure silvery white Patna onions, and steep them in boiling water, changing the water three or four times, every ten minutes; drain away all the water and add the onions to the soup; boil, and serve up hot.

112.—Bridal Soup, or Soup Elegant.

Take two large shoulders of veal; cut them up small, bones and all, and, after washing thoroughly, boil over a brisk fire, with *white* pepper and the best white salt. Be careful that the scum that rises is well skimmed; reduce the fire, and allow it to simmer until the meat falls off the bones; strain the soup, let it cool, and then thoroughly free it of all fat; return it into a clean digester, add more salt and white pepper if necessary, and some *white* stocks of celery; boil it, and clear it with the whites of two eggs well beaten up; strain through flannel and set aside.

Take the best and most transparent parts of a calf's head and the tongue, and boil perfectly tender without reducing them to shreds, being careful to remove all the scum that rises to the surface; lay the boiled tongue and meat out on a clean dish; slice the tongue fine, and cut out all manner of devices, such as, diamonds, squares, circles, hearts, stars, &c.; do the same with the best and cleanest parts of meat selected from the head; take care that no particles of scum or other impurities be adhering to them; where any does adhere, rinse it off in a little of the cleared soup; then place them carefully into the tureen in which it is purposed to serve up the soup. If fancy macaroni be procurable, a table-spoonful may be boiled tender, free of all particles of dust or powder, and added to the cut-up meat and tongue, over which pour the boiling-hot soup; add to it a wineglassful of the palest sherry, and serve up hot.

N.B.—The calf's tongue and meat of the head may be boiled with the veal, but they should be removed when tender, and not allowed to dissolve with the longer simmering of the veal.

This is an elegant soup, beautifully transparent, and of the colour of light champagne.

113.—Soup Royal.

Take a shin of beef, the best parts of meat cut off from a calf's head, and the tongue; cut the beef into small particles, but leave the tongue and the meat from the calf's head whole; add pepper and salt, and boil well, clearing the scum as it rises; remove the tongue and the meat of the calf's head when sufficiently tender, but continue to boil the shin of beef until it is well dissolved; then strain it, and cut away all the fat; put it up again with plenty of soup herbs, and more salt and pepper if necessary; boil it well up; squeeze into the soup the juice of half a lemon, and skim it well; strain it once more, and set it aside.

Cut the tongue into slices of an eighth of an inch thick, trim them into the shape of large diamonds, and set aside. Cut up the meat of the calf's head into one-inch squares and strips of an inch and a half long and half an inch wide; add to these a few ready-fried circular flat brain cakes, make also a few egg balls and forcemeat balls, and, after cooking, add them to the rest of the meat, tongue, &c., and set aside.

Take four red carrots, one pound of green peas, half a pound of boiled potatoes, one large turnip, one large Patna onion, a quarter of a pound of roasted and ground split peas or gram dal, some soup herbs, pepper, and salt, the pulp of one orange, and the peels of half an orange and half a lemon. Put these into a stewpan with water sufficient to cover the whole; boil them thoroughly, skimming all the while; when perfectly dissolved, turn them out into a colander and allow all the water to drain away; then turn the contents of the colander into a sieve, and pass the vegetables, &c., through it, rejecting all such as will not pass. Add the whole or a part of the strained vegetables to the soup, which should not be thicker in consistency than a good thick potato soup.

Next stew one dozen good French prunes in a claret-glassful of port wine, which also strain through a sieve, rejecting stones, &c., and add the strained portion to the soup; then boil the whole, strain it once more, add to it all the forcemeat and egg balls, the brain cakes, tongue, &c., and serve up, adding to it more salt, wine, or sauce, if needed.

N.B.—This soup properly made is without its equal.

FISH.

114.—Fish Mooloo.

Fry the fish and let it cool. Scrape a cocoanut, put a teacupful of hot water into it, rub it well, strain it and put aside; then put two spoonfuls more of water; strain this also; cut up three or four green chilies, and as many onions as you like, with half a garlic. Fry them with a little ghee, and whilst frying put the last straining of the cocoanut water in with the ingredients till it is dry; then add the first water of the nut, and pour the whole over the fish, with some vinegar, ginger, whole pepper, and salt to your taste.

115.—*Another Way.*

Fry in a little ghee three or four chilies cut up, half a clove of garlic, and some sliced onions. When half fried, add two tablespoonfuls of cocoanut milk, and continue to fry until dry; then stir into it a teacupful of cocoanut milk, a little vinegar, some sliced ginger, peppercorns, and salt to taste, and while hot pour it over a cold fried or boiled fish.

116.—*Another Way.*

Cut up a fish into small two-inch squares, and fry in ghee, with egg, bread-crumbs, and turmeric, of a nice brown colour. Boil in cocoanut milk some sliced green ginger and sliced green chilies; then add the fish, with salt to taste, and let it stew until the sauce has thickened. Serve up hot.

117.—Prawn Cutlet.

Shell and wash the prawns; remove the heads, but leave the tails; slit them down in the centre, and gently beat them flat with a rolling-pin; sprinkle them with pepper and salt, and some finely-minced soup herbs; rub them over with yolk of eggs, and dredge with flour; fry over a very moderate fire to a rich light brown colour. Garnish the dish with fried green parsley, or serve up with tomato sauce gravy as per recipe No. 300.

118.—Crabs in Shell.

Clean and boil the crabs in salt; remove them out of the shells; pick and clean them well, and reserve the coral for dressing.

Chop and mince fine the crabs; add some onion and ginger juice, a little lime-juice, pepper, and salt, and a little mushroom catsup. Melt some butter, and fry the mixture in it until the butter be absorbed; then add a little stock, and remove from the fire immediately the stock begins to dry. Butter the shells, and fill with the mixture. The meat of six crabs will refill five shells. Take some finely-sifted bread-crumbs; grind down the coral, and put it over the mixture on the shells, with the bread-crumbs, and bits of butter; bake for a few minutes.

119.—Tamarind Fish.

Make a thick pickle of ripe tamarinds, good English vinegar, and a little salt; pass through a seive, rejecting all stones and fibres. Select really good fresh hilsa fish, full size, with roes. Remove all the scales and fins, cut away the heads and tails, remove the roes, clean out the fish inside, and then slice up, an inch thick. Wipe away all blood, &c., with a clean dry towel. Care must be taken to use no water in the cleaning of the fish or in the preparation of the pickle. The board on which the fish is cut up, and also the knife, must be very clean. After all the blood, &c., has been thoroughly cleaned and wiped away, lay out the slices of fish and roe on a clean dish, sprinkle thickly with salt, and place over them a wire dish-cover to keep away the flies. Four or five hours afterwards put a layer of the pickle into a wide-mouthed bottle or jar, and a thick coating of pickle over each slice of fish and the roes, after washing away the salt with a little vinegar; lay them in order in the jar, until the last of the fish is put in; then be careful to put in a very thick layer of the pickle. Cork the jar securely, and tie it down with a good bladder to keep it air-tight, and in three weeks it will be fit for use. It is desirable to fill each jar well up to the mouth, to effect which the jars or bottles to be selected should be of the required size.

N.B.—If the fish be really fresh, all the ingredients of good quality, and no water be used in the operation of cleaning and pickling, the jars well filled, and mouths secured with sound bladder, the fish will keep good for months, and will be fit to send home.

120 -Smoked Fish.

The mango fish, beckty, or hilsa should be cut down the back, spread open, and well washed and salted. Have a bright charcoal fire, and sprinkle over it some bran, with brown sugar; cover the fire with an open-work bamboo basket, having over it a coarse duster; arrange the fish over the duster, and allow them to smoke. When one side has browned, turn and brown the other side. As the smoke decreases, add more bran, and fan up the fire. A duster thrown over the fish while smoking will facilitate the operation.

121.—Dried Prawns.

Strip the prawns of their shells; keep them for a day in salt mixed with turmeric; then string and put them out in the sun daily for fifteen or twenty days.

122.—Prawn Powder.

Take a seer of dry prawns; wash them well, dry over the fire until crisp, pound fine, with some red pepper and nutmeg, pass through a sieve, and bottle for use. A teaspoonful spread over bread and butter is considered a relish.

JOINTS, MADE DISHES, ETC.

123.—Corned Round of Beef.

Select a good round of beef four days previously to its being required for the table, together with two seers of cooking salt, eight fresh juicy limes, one anna-worth of saltpetre, and a tablespoonful of suckur, a description of moist brown sugar. Pound fine the saltpetre; put the rind of four limes, pared fine, into a marble mortar, with a tablespoonful of brandy or other spirit; bruise and pound it well, adding to it the suckur or brown sugar, and gradually half the powdered saltpetre; mix all well together. Take one seer of the salt, and mix into it the contents of the marble mortar; divide the mixture into four equal parts, and rub briskly one-fourth part of it into the round; puncture the beef lightly during the operation with a clean bright steel sailmaker's needle, to allow the mixture to penetrate more freely. An hour or two after take another fourth part of the mixture; squeeze into it the juice of the four limes from which the rind had been removed, and repeat the operation of rubbing it into the round, puncturing it lightly with the needle; turn the beef over from side to side continually, so that one side do not soak or steep more in the brine than another; repeat the operation of rubbing it well several times during the day. Next morning place it on a dry dish, and rub into it another fourth part of the prepared salt; let it stand for an hour or so, then pour over it the old brine; repeat the rubbing two or three times during the day, turning the beef continually. On the third day rub half of the remaining saltpetre into the beef dry, and allow it to stand for an hour or two; then add the rest of the saltpetre and the juice of the four limes to the remaining fourth part of the mixture, in which keep turning and rubbing the beef during the day as before; in the evening pour over it the stale brine, cover it thickly with the one seer of remaining salt, and place a heavy weight upon it, until required to be boiled the next day.

124.—Beef a la Mode.

Corn a round of beef in every particular as directed above, and twenty-four hours previously to its being cooked lard it as follows with the undermentioned ingredients:—Four pounds of lard or fat bacon, half a tablespoonful of cinnamon powdered, half a seer or one pound of finely-powdered pepper, one tablespoonful of cloves powdered, and four tablespoonfuls of chutnee strained through muslin. Mix the ground pepper, ground hot spices, and strained chutnee with a claret-glassful of mixed sauces, such as Harvey, walnut, Worcestershire, tap, tomato, &c. Cut up into long narrow slips the lard or bacon to correspond in thickness with the larding-pin, and lay the slips into the mixture of spices, sauces, &c., for an hour or two before larding the beef, which should be larded through and through, and as closely as possible.

Cook it the next day, either in plain water, with half a pint of vinegar, and with bay-leaves and peppercorns, as is usual, or in a preparation of claret or champagne with vinegar, bay-leaves, &c. This is not necessary, but it tends to the improvement of the flavour at some considerable cost.

125.—Le Fricandeau de Veau.

Take a large leg of veal; remove the knuckle-bone; corn and lard it in all respects like a beef à la mode, reducing the ingredients in proportion to the difference in size and weight between a round of beef and the leg of veal. Boil, baste, and glaze it well in the liquor in which it is boiled. Serve up with all sorts of boiled and glazed vegetables.

126.—Hunter's Beef, or Spiced Beef.

Corn a round of beef, as per recipe No. 123, with the addition of large quantities of finely-powdered pepper and hot spices. Some of the pepper and spice should be well rubbed in with the saltpetre, and the beef should be punctured well the whole time with a needle to insure the saltpetre and spices penetrating. After the dry saltpetre and spice have been well rubbed in, prepare a mixture of salt, saltpetre, suckr, lemon-rind, pepper, and spice, and rub in one-fourth of the mixture, continuing to puncture the beef. Add subsequently to the brine the juice of lemon, and observe closely all the instructions given in recipe No. 123. On the seventh day remove the beef from the brine; rub it well with two tablespoonfuls of finely-powdered spices and pepper; inclose it thoroughly in skins of fat, and then in a strong coarse pie-crust, and bake it in a good oven. A baker's oven is the best.

127.—Collared Brisket.

Bone a brisket of beef; rub into it saltpetre, suckur or brown sugar, and one seer of salt, with some lime-juice; keep it in the brine for thirty-six hours, rubbing it continually. Then remove it from the brine, and clear away all the salt. Roll the beef tightly into a collar, secure it well, inclose it in a stout duster, and boil it.

128.—Spiced Collared Brisket.

The process is the same as the above, but if the beef be required to keep for any lengthened time the quantity of salt ought to be doubled, the beef kept in the brine for seventy-two hours, and hot spices, pepper, chutnee, and sauces added. The beef after being rolled should be packed in the skin of fat, then in a coarse pastry, instead of in plaintain-leaf, and baked in a baker's oven.

129.—Pigeons with Petit Pois.

Kill and feather, without plunging into hot water, four young, full-grown pigeons, taking care not to break their skins; singe them, to destroy any remaining feathers; then wash them in three or four cold waters, cut them in halves, dredge them well with salt and finely-sifted pepper, and allow to remain for an hour. Then boil up two tablespoonfuls of ghee or lard, and fry the birds to a rich brown, turning them over. When sufficiently browned, put in a cupful of beef stock, and allow to simmer until the birds are quite tender; pour over them a tin of petit pois with their gravy, and serve up hot.

130.—Ducks with Green Olives.

Choose young, full-grown, tender ducks; feather and singe them as directed in the foregoing recipe, after which wash them in three or four cold waters; stuff the ducks according to recipe No. 325, and bake in a deep dish in a moderate oven until brown; then add a good beef stock with sliced onions, and bake until the stock is reduced; remove the ducks, and put into the pan the contents of a bottle of olives stoned, and allow to bake for ten or fifteen minutes to soften the olives; place the ducks on a clean dish, arrange the olives round the ducks, and pour the gravy over. Serve up hot.

131.—Kidney Stew.

Steep in lukewarm water for a few minutes a dozen mutton kidneys, and remove the white skin or coat which will become perceptible; cut into halves or quarter them, wash in three or four waters, and allow them to remain as long as possible in pepper, salt, and the juice of onions, ginger, and garlic; boil up three dessertspoonfuls of ghee or lard in a deep frying-pan, throw in the kidneys with the juice, put in half a clove of garlic, and cover over the whole with eight large Patna onions sliced each into eight slices, and separated so as to cover over the whole surface of the pan; pour over it as much hot stock as will keep all the onions under, and simmer over a slow fire until the onions disappear, when serve up quite hot.

132.—French Mutton Chops.

Take half a dozen chops cut from a breast of mutton, throwing away the intermediate bones—that is to say, allow the meat of two chops to remain on one bone. Wash, dry, and steep the chops for an hour or two before dinner in the juice of onions, ginger, and garlic—say four teaspoonfuls of the first to three of the second and two of the last. Mix on a large board pepper, salt, and flour, with which dredge the chops thoroughly, and fry quickly in boiling ghee or lard, taking care in turning over and removing the chops not to use a fork or anything likely to occasion any wound to the chops, which should be held by the bones with a pair of pincers. Serve up hot immediately they have become of a good rich brown colour.

133.—Mutton Stew.

Cut up a breast of mutton in the usual way for a stew; wash and dry the meat. Take of the juice of onions one tablespoonful, of ginger half a tablespoonful, and of garlic a quarter of a tablespoonful; mix with the meat, add pepper and salt, and allow to stand for any time from one to four hours.

Fry in a large stewpan two tablespoonfuls of ghee or lard, and when on the boil fry to a nice brown all the meat only; afterwards pour in the liquor in which the meat had been steeped, and allow to simmer for fifteen or twenty minutes; thicken some stock with a teaspoonful of flour, and add it to the stew; allow to simmer until the meat is perfectly tender.

If vegetables be required (the addition of which, however, is not considered any improvement), the original gravy, before adding the stock, must be removed and set aside.

Let the vegetables, consisting of, say, potatoes, carrots, turnips, and cut-up and sliced cabbage, after being cleaned, remain for an hour or two in cold water; lay them over the meat, and pour in hot stock sufficient to cover the whole of the meat and vegetables, and allow to simmer over a brisk coal fire until quite tender; then pour into the pot the original gravy which had been removed, and serve up hot.

Or, instead of the vegetables named above, take only twenty-five or thirty tamatoes, in which case the stock should be lessened, as the tomatoes produce a large amount of liquid, and do not require as much boiling as the harder vegetables.

134.—Mutton Brains and Love Apples.

Take six brains, sixteen to twenty large tomatoes, two chittacks or four ounces of butter, and eight biscuits. Wash the brains well; clean, boil, and halve, or cut each into three pieces; thoroughly butter the dish which will be put on the table; dredge it well with finely-powdered biscuit; lay in the brains; cut the tomatoes, and lay them in the dish between the brains, the cut ends upwards; add a small cupful of good stock, and, after sprinkling a sufficient quantity of pepper and salt as a seasoning, dredge thickly over with the ground biscuit-powder, and bake of a rich brown. Serve up hot.

135.—Kid Roasted Whole.

Bespeak from a butcher a whole kid, with its head on.

Prepare a stuffing as per recipe No. 323 or 325, and after cleaning the kid, stuff into it the stuffing; break the joints of the legs, and fold and truss them like a pig; then put it up to roast, basting it the whole time with beef suet melted down, to which add hot water and salt. Serve up in a sitting posture like a pig, and with a lime in the mouth.

136.—Potato Pie.

Boil and mash down some potatoes, with pepper, salt, milk, and butter; line a pie-dish a quarter of an inch thick with the mash; arrange in it a nicely-browned mutton, beef, or chicken stew, cover it over with a thick coat of the mashed potatoes, and bake for a quarter of an hour.

137.—Minced Veal Potato Pie.

Make a good rich veal mince, mixed with a little ham, and some sippets of bread-crumb cut into small squares, diamonds, &c., and fried in butter; line the pie-dish with mashed potatoes as above directed; fill into it the veal mince, with plenty of gravy; arrange the sippets, cover over with a thick crust of the mashed potatoes, and bake for a quarter of an hour.

138.—Beef Steak and Pigeon Pie.

This should consist of a slice of good steak, two pounds of beef, one chittack or two ounces of ghee, a teaspoonful of salt, two fresh limes, four young pigeons, twelve oysters, twelve curry onions cut lengthways into fine slices, a teaspoonful of ground pepper, some sweet herbs, and a dessertspoonful of flour.

Cut up the steak into pieces three inches long, and two inches or two and a half wide, by half an inch thick. Cut and divide each pigeon into four pieces; put up two pounds of beef with sufficient water to make a good strong gravy, throwing in all the scraggy parts and other rejections of the steak and pigeons. Warm the ghee, and fry in it the sliced onions; throw in, well dredged with the flour, the steaks and pigeons, and after frying a while add the pepper, salt, soup herbs, and some of the rind of the limes, and about half the beef gravy. Set the whole on a slow fire, and simmer until the meat is tender; allow to cool; then add the oysters and the remaining gravy, with the juice of two limes; put into a dish lined with pastry, cover over the whole with a pastry crust, and bake.

139.—Veal Pie.

Cut a leg of veal into small pieces, or a breast into chops, and parboil in water enough to fill the pie-dish. When about half stewed take the veal out; season the gravy with pepper, salt, a little mace, and a little bacon; dredge in a little flour; line the sides of the dish with a pie-crust; arrange the meat, pour in the gravy, cover it with a pie-crust, and bake it for an hour.

140.—Macaroni Pie.

Take half a pound of macaroni (recipe No. 218); boil and throw away the first water; then boil it again in some milk, and remove when it is quite tender. Prepare a strong gravy or soup with two pounds of beef, well seasoned with ground white pepper, salt, and soup herbs.

Bruise into fine powder two ounces of some good English cheese; take a dessertspoonful of very dry mustard, half a teaspoonful of very finely powdered white pepper, about two teaspoonfuls of salt, and two chittacks or four ounces of butter. Pound very fine a couple of crisp biscuits.

Pour over the boiled macaroni sufficient beef gravy or stock to entirely cover it; then put in all the pepper, salt, and mustard, but only half the ground cheese. Set it to simmer over a slow fire until the gravy begins to dry, and the macaroni acquires some consistency. Then with three ounces of butter (free of water) butter well the baking-dish; pou rinto it the macaroni; mix the remaining ground cheese with the powdered biscuit, and strew it over the pie; cut into small pieces the remaining ounce of butter, and throw that also over the pie; then put the dish into an oven, and bake to a fine light but rich brown colour. Ten to fifteen minutes' baking will be sufficient.

141.—Alderman's Mock Turtle Pie.

Make an extra rich hash of a calf's head, cutting the pieces from the cheeks two and a half to three inches long, and one and three-quarters to two inches wide. Slice the tongue, and cut into large-sized shapes. Prepare brain cakes, and plenty of forcemeat and egg balls as per recipes Nos. 289 to 295.

Make an extra strong stock with eight calves' feet; season it highly with soup herbs, salt, and plenty of ground black pepper; simmer until the meat begins to drop away from the bones; strain through a coarse sieve, in order to get a very thick stock, passing as much of the dissolved meat through as possible.

Line a deep pie-dish with a thick and rich pie-pastry, and arrange in it the hash, egg and meat balls, and brain cakes, with some twenty or thirty green leaves of spinach, cut up to about the size and shape of the meat. Pour over the whole as much stock as will fill the dish, cover over with pastry, and bake.

142.—Sauce for Alderman's Mock Turtle Pie.

Mix with some of the stock the contents of a canister of oysters well bruised, the pulp of sixteen or twenty prunes, a blade of mace, some nutmeg and cloves, a wineglassful of port wine, and a tablespoonful of Worcestershire sauce; allow to simmer for ten minutes, and add it to the ready-baked pie before it is put on the table.

143.—Friar Tuck's Mock Venison Pastry Pie.

Take the chop ends of two large fat breasts of mutton; remove the bones, and after the meat has been washed, cleaned, and dried, lard well with narrow slips of lean bacon and corned tongue; then cut it up into twelve well-shaped chops nicely trimmed; steep them in the juice of onions, ginger, and garlic in the proportion of one tablespoonful of the former to a dessertspoonful of the latter, and half a teaspoonful of the last.

Make a strong broth or stock of the other side of the mutton, and all the rejections of bones, &c.; season it well with pepper, salt, and soup herbs; remove the scum and cut away all the fat; then strain through a sieve, rejecting all the fat, but passing through some of the lean; allow it to simmer until it thickens, then add to it two blades of mace, half a dozen allspice, and as many small sticks of cinnamon.

Line a deep metal pie-dish with the pastry pie-crust as per recipe No. 200, reserving sufficient for the upper crust. Prepare a sausage roll, say six inches long, and two inches and a quarter thick, of minced veal and udder, using the ordinary pie-crust pastry to inclose it in; then slice it into twelve equal slices of the thickness of half an inch.

Remove the twelve chops out of the onion, garlic, and ginger juice; dredge them well with finely-sifted flour mixed with pepper and salt; heat in a large deep frying-pan four tablespoonfuls of lard; fry the chops of a light brown colour, and remove them carefully; then dredge with flour and slightly brown the twelve slices of sausage, six of which lay at the bottom of the pie-dish; lay over them six of the mutton chops; over the mutton chops place another layer of the sliced sausage roll, and over that the remaining six chops; pour in as much of the stock or gravy as will fill the pie-dish, cover it over with a layer of the pastry as per recipe No. 200, and bake carefully.

144.—Sauce for Friar Tuck's Mock Venison Pastry Pie.

Put some of the stock or gravy into the pan in which the chops and sliced sausages had been browned; add two tablespoonfuls of bruised and powdered oysters, and simmer from ten to fifteen minutes. Serve hot, on the pie being cut, adding at the last moment a wineglassful of port wine and one tablespoonful of lime-juice.

Make a hole in the centre of the pie through the crusts, and pour in the sauce with the help of a lipped sauce-boat.

145.—Leg of Mutton Dumpling.

Prepare a good pie-crust with one seer and a quarter of soojee, half a seer of flour, and half a seer of suet, as per recipe No. 199.

Clean and trim the leg, cutting away the end of the knuckle-bone, and any other projections likely to injure the dumpling. Sprinkle it well with ground pepper and some salt, and confine it securely in the pastry, closing all joinings with the aid of a little water. Place the dumpling into a strong napkin, previously buttered and dredged with flower; tie it securely, and allow it to boil from three to four hours. Care must be taken that during the whole process of boiling the dumpling remains suspended in the water, and not resting on the bottom of the pan. On removing it from the boiler, plunge it immediately into a large tureen of cold water for two or three minutes. This will strengthen the pastry and prevent its bursting or breaking while it is being served up.

146.—Sausage Rolls.

Take equal portions of cold roast veal and ham, or cold fowl and tongue; chop them together very small; season with a teaspoonful of powdered sweet herbs, and a spoonful of mixed salt and cayenne pepper; mix well together. Put three tablespoonfuls of the meat well rolled together into enough pastry (pie-crust recipe No. 199) to cover it.

When you have used up the whole of your materials, bake them for half an hour in a brisk oven. These rolls are excellent eating, either hot or cold, and are especially adapted for travelling, gipsy, boating, or pic-nic parties.

147.—Dumpode Goose (Indian Way).

Take a good fat tender goose; feather, clean, and bone it carefully without destroying the skin; when every bone has been removed, pour into the goose a mixture composed of a dessertspoonful each of mustard, sweet oil, and mixed sauces.

Take all the bones and the giblet, the liver excepted, and make a good gravy seasoned with pepper, salt, soup herbs, and bay-leaves. Mince very fine three pounds of beef, a quarter of a pound of beef suet, a quarter of a pound of fat bacon, and the liver of the goose. Take of chopped garden herbs a tablespoonful, powdered black pepper a dessertspoonful, mixed hot spices finely powdered a dessertspoonful, finely-grated bread-crumbs two tablespoonfuls, salt a dessertspoonful, and essence of anchovies, if liked, one teaspoonful. Mix the above well together, and stuff the goose.

Melt two chittacks and a half or five ounces of ghee; put in the goose, and pour over it the soup made of the bones and giblet, and allow it to stew until quite tender; then glace the goose, as also some boiled turnips, carrots, onions, and potatoes, and serve up hot, surrounded with the vegetables and some English pickles.

148.—Dumpode Duck (Eastern Way).

Take a good fat duck; feather, clean, and bone it without hurting the skin; pour into it a mixture made up of a teaspoonful each of mustard, sweet oil, and mixed sauce.

Make a gravy of the bones and giblet, seasoning it with pepper, salt, soup herbs, and a few bay-leaves.

Mince together with the liver of the duck two pounds and a half of good beef, half a pound of beef suet, a dessertspoonful of chopped garden herbs, a tablespoonful of grated bread-crumbs, half a teaspoonful of mixed hot spices pounded, a teaspoonful each of black pepper and salt, and, for those who like it, half a teaspoonful of essence of anchovies. Mix these well together, and stuff the duck. Melt one chittack and a half or three ounces of ghee; put in the duck; pour over it the giblet gravy, and allow it to cook until tender; then glace the duck, as also some ready-boiled mixed vegetables, and serve up, surrounding the duck with the vegetables and some hot West-Indian pickle.

149.—Fowl a la Cardinal, or Dumpode Capon or Fowl.

Feather the bird, clean it, and remove every bone very carefully without injuring the skin.

Make a good strong broth or gravy of the bone and giblet, reserving the liver.

Pour into the bird a mixture of sweet oil, mustard, and sauces in the proportion of one teaspoonful of each.

Mince the liver together with one pound and a half of good beef, one pound and a half of beef suet, a dessertspoonful each of finely-chopped garden herbs and finely-grated bread-crumbs, a teaspoonful each of powdered mixed hot spices, finely-powdered black pepper, and salt, if liked, and half a dozen oysters. Mix all well together, and stuff the bird; melt two chittacks or four ounces of ghee, add to it the giblet gravy, cook and glace the bird in it, as also some vegetables, and serve up hot, adding a little cayenne pepper to the gravy to make it piquant

150.—Brisket of Beef Trambland.

Heat or melt in a saucepan two chittacks of butter free of water; fry to a light brown a tablespoonful of finely-sliced onions, then add a tablespoonful and a half of flour, which must be put in very gradually, stirring the whole time; add half a teaspoonful of ground pepper, and one teaspoonful of salt. When these have been well mixed, pour in gradually a large cupful of pure milk, and lastly two wineglassfuls of vinegar. Keep stirring to prevent the sauce lumping, Mince fine half a dozen pickled gherkins or French beans, and mince up also the yolks and whites of six hard-boiled eggs. Boil a fresh brisket of beef, and dish up quite hot. Pour over it the sauce, over which sprinkle the minced pickle, and then cover the whole with the minced eggs.

151.—Mutton Trambland

Is prepared, in all respects, as the above. The joint best adapted to "trambland" is a fore-quarter, or only the shoulder, or the breast if required for a small party of two or three.

152.—Bubble and Squeak.

Put into a pot cold meat cut into thin slices two inches square, with ready-boiled peas, cauliflower, cabbage, potatoes, turnips, and carrots cut up, with pepper, salt, and sliced ginger, and with as much good stock as will cover the meat and vegetables; allow the whole to simmer until the meat and vegetables have absorbed half the stock, when it will be ready. Serve it up bubbling and squeaking.

153.—To Stew a Fillet of Veal.

Bone, lard, and stuff a fillet of veal; half roast, and then stew it with two quarts of white stock, a teaspoonful of lemon pickle, and one of mushroom catsup. Before serving, strain the gravy; thicken it with butter rolled in flour; add a little cayenne, salt, and some pickled mushrooms; heat it, and pour it over the veal. Have ready two or three dozens of forcemeat balls to put round it and upon the top. Garnish with cut lemon.

154.—Veal Cutlets.

Cut a neck of veal into cutlets, or take them off a leg. Season two well-beaten eggs with pounded mace, nutmeg, salt, pepper, and finely-chopped sweet marjoram, lemon, thyme, and parsley; dip the cutlets into it; sift over them grated bread, and fry them in clarified butter. Serve with a white sauce, forcemeat balls, and small mushrooms. Garnish with fried parsley.

155.—Kidney Toasts.

Pound, in a marble mortar, the kidney and the surrounding fat; season with pepper, salt, grated lemon-peel, and nutmeg; mix with it the yolk of an egg well beaten; lay it upon thin toasted bread cut into square bits; put a little butter into a dish, lay in it the kidney toasts, and brown them in an oven. Serve them very hot.

156.—Rolled Mutton.

Bone a shoulder of mutton carefully, so as not to injure the skin; cut all the meat from the skin, mince it small, and season it highly with pepper, nutmeg, and a clove, some parsley, lemon, thyme, sweet marjoram chopped, and a pounded onion, all well mixed, together with the well-beaten yolk of an egg; roll it up very tightly in the skin; tie it round, and bake it in an oven for two or three hours, according to the size of the mutton. Make a gravy of the bones and parings; season with an onion, pepper, and salt; strain and thicken it with flour and butter; add a tablespoonful each of vinegar, mushroom catsup, soy, and lemon pickle, and a teacupful of port wine; garnish with forcemeat balls made of grated bread, and part of the mince.

157.—Haggis.

Wash and clean the heart and lights; parboil and mince them very small; add one pound of minced suet, two or three large onions minced, and two small handfuls of oatmeal; season highly with pepper and salt, and mix all well together: the bag being perfectly clean and sweet, put in the ingredients; press out the air, sew it up, and boil it for three hours.

158.—To Boil Marrow-bones.

Saw them even at the bottom; butter and flour some bits of linen, and tie a piece over the top of each bone; boil them for an hour or two; take off the linen, and serve them with thin slices of dry toast cut into square bits. At table the marrow should be put upon the toast, and a little pepper and salt sprinkled over it.

159.—Beef or Mutton Baked with Potatoes.

Boil some potatoes; peel and pound them in a mortar with one or two small onions; moisten them with milk and an egg beaten up; add a little salt and pepper. Season slices of beef or mutton chops with salt and pepper, and more onion, if the flavour is approved; rub the bottom of a pudding-dish with butter, and put in a layer of the mashed potatoes, which should be as thick as a batter, and then a layer of meat, and so on alternately, till the dish is filled, ending with potatoes. Bake in an oven for one hour.

160.—Olive Royals.

Boil one pound of potatoes, and when nearly cold rub them perfectly smooth with four ounces of flour and one ounce of butter; knead all together till it becomes a paste; roll it out about a quarter of an inch thick, cut it into rounds, and lay upon one side any sort of cold roasted meat cut into thin small bits, and seasoned with pepper and salt; put a small bit of butter over the meat; wet the edges of the paste, and close it in the form of half-circles. Fry them in boiling fresh dripping till of a light brown colour; lay them before the fire, on the back of a sieve, to drain. Serve them with or without gravy in the dish. For a change, mince the meat, and season it as before directed. The potatoes should be very mealy.

161.—To Boil Ox-Cheek.

Wash half a head very clean; let it lie in cold water for some hours; break the bone in two, taking care not to break the flesh; put it into a pot of boiling water, and let it boil from two to three hours; take out the bone. Serve it with boiled carrots and turnips. The liquor in which the head has been boiled may be strained, and made into barley broth.

162.—To Stew Ox-Cheek.

Clean the head as before directed, and parboil it; take out the bone; stew it in part of the liquor in which it was boiled, thickened with a piece of butter mixed with flour, and browned. Cut into dice, or into any fancy shape, as many carrots and turnips as will fill a pint basin. Mince two or three onions, add the vegetables, and season with salt and pepper. Cover the pan closely, and stew it two hours. A little before serving, add a glassful of port wine.

163.—Dressed Ox-Cheek.

Prepare it as directed for stewing; cut the meat into square pieces; make a sauce with a quart of good gravy, thickened with butter mixed with flour; season with salt and pepper, a little cayenne, and a table-spoonful of vinegar; put in the head, and simmer it till quite tender. A few minutes before serving add a little catsup or white wine. Force-meat balls may be added.

164.—Potted Ox-Cheek

May be made of the meat that is left from any one of the above dishes. It is cut into small bits, and heated up with a little of the liquor in which the cheek was boiled, seasoned with pepper, salt, nutmeg, and a little vinegar, then put into a mould, and turned out when required for use. It is used for supper or luncheon, and is eaten with mustard and vinegar.

165.—Breasts of Mutton a la Ste. Menoult.

Stew them with carrots, onions, and spices in gravy, and when done drain them and take out the bones; flatten the meat between two dishes, and when cold cut it into the form of cutlets or hearts; brush them with the beaten yolk of an egg; roll them in grated bread, then in clarified butter, and again in the grated bread. Bake them in an oven till of a fine brown colour, and serve them with an Italian or any other sauce.

166.—To Cure Mutton Ham.

Cut a hind quarter of good mutton into the shape of a ham; pound one ounce of saltpetre, with one pound of coarse salt and a quarter of a pound of brown sugar; rub the ham well with this mixture, taking care to stuff the hole of the shank well with salt and sugar, and let it lie a fortnight, rubbing it well with the pickle every two or three days; then take it out and press it with a weight for one day; smoke it with saw-dust for ten or fifteen days, or hang it to dry in the kitchen. If the ham is to be boiled soon after it has been smoked, soak it one hour; and if it has been smoked any length of time, it will require to be soaked several hours. Put it on in cold water and boil it gently two hours. It is eaten cold at breakfast, luncheon, or supper. A mutton ham is sometimes cured with the above quantity of salt and sugar, with the addition of half an ounce of pepper, a quarter of an ounce of cloves, and one nutmeg.

167.—Meat or Birds in Jelly.

Clean the meat or the bird or birds; fully roast, bake, or stew in the usual way.

Place the meat in the mould, or if birds, arrange them with their breasts downwards; fill the mould quite full with the jelly, recipe No. 329; set it to cool till the next day; then turn it on a dish, breasts upwards. Garnish the dish with curled parsley, and some of the jelly cut fine, and sprinkled about.

If the jelly be clear, it will form a handsome side-dish for dinner or supper.

168.—Pigeons in Savoury Jelly.

Bone six pigeons; remove the heads and feet, stuff with sausage-meat, and roast; lay the pigeons in a mould with the breasts down; fill up the mould with jelly, recipe No. 329; and when cold, turn out. Garnish with parsley, and some of the jelly cut fine, and sprinkled round the dish.

VEGETABLES.

All vegetables should be boiled quickly, and, with the exception of spinach, in an open vessel, skimming them carefully.

Herbs of all sorts should be gathered when in flower, and on a dry day, and, being well cleaned from dust and dirt, tied up in small bunches and dried before the fire. They may then be kept in paper bags labelled; or rubbed to a powder, sifted, and put into bottles and labelled.

169.—To Boil Potatoes.

Wash and pare them, throwing them into cold water as they are pared; put them into a saucepan, cover them with cold water, and throw in a little salt; cover the saucepan closely, and let them boil quickly for half an hour; pour off the water immediately, and set the pan by the side of the fire to dry the potatoes.

170.—*Another Way.*

Wash them very clean, put them on in cold water, cover the saucepan, and let them boil quickly; as soon as the water boils pour it off, and cover them with cold water; add a little salt, and when the water boils pour it off instantly, when the potatoes will be sufficiently done; dry them, and take off the skins before serving.

171.—To Broil Boiled Potatoes.

After boiling potatoes not quite sufficiently to send to table, put them on a gridiron over a clear fire, and turn them frequently till they are of a nice brown colour all over; serve them hot; take care they do not become too hard, as that spoils the flavour.

172.—To Brown Potatoes under Meat while Roasting.

After being boiled, lay them on a dish, and place it in the dripping-pan; baste them now and then with a little of the meat dripping, and when one side is browned turn the other; they should all be of an equal colour.

173.—Potato Ribbons.

Wash four or five large potatoes, scrape them, and cut them into thin strips round and round, keeping as nearly to one width as possible; throw them into cold water as they are cut, and then fry them of a light brown, in very hot or boiling beef dripping; strew over them a little salt and pepper, and before serving, drain them upon a dish turned up before the fire.

174.—To Boil Turnips.

Wash, pare, and throw them into cold water; put them on in boiling water with a little salt, and boil them from two hours to two and a half;

drain them in a colander, put them into a saucepan, and, mixing in a bit of butter, with a beater mash them very smoothly; add half a pint of milk, mix it well with the turnips, and make them quite hot before serving. If they are to be served plain, dish them as soon as the water is drained off.

175.—To Dress Young Turnips.

Wash, peel, and boil them till tender in water with a little salt; serve them with melted butter poured over them. Or,

They may be stewed in a pint of milk thickened with a bit of butter rolled in flour, and seasoned with salt and pepper, and served with the sauce.

176.—To Boil Spinach.

Pick it very carefully, and wash it thoroughly two or three times in plenty of cold water; then put it on in boiling water with a little salt; let it boil nearly twenty minutes; put it into a colander, hold it under the water-cock, and let the water run on it for a minute; put it into a saucepan, beat it perfectly smooth with a beater or wooden spoon, add a bit of butter and three tablespoonfuls of cream, mix it well together, and make it hot before serving. When dished, it is scored in squares with the back of a knife.

177.—*Another Way.*

After being nicely picked and well washed, put it into a saucepan, with no more water than adheres to it; add a little salt; cover the pan closely, and boil it till tender, frequently shaking it; beat it quite smooth, adding butter and cream, and make it quite hot. Spinach may be served with poached eggs, or fried sausages laid on it.

When the spinach is bitter, it is preferable to boil it in water.

178.—To Boil Cauliflowers.

Trim them neatly, and let them lie an hour or two in cold water; then rinse them in fresh cold water, and put them with a very little salt into boiling water; boil them twenty minutes, or half an hour if very large. They may be boiled in milk and water, and require to be skimmed with particular attention.

179.—To Boil French Beans.

Cut off the stalk and string them; if not very young, cut them in four, or into very thin slices; put them into water as they are done, and put them on in boiling water, with a little salt, and let them boil for half an hour. If they are old they will require a longer time to boil. Melted butter in a sauce-tureen is served with them.

180.—To Boil Asparagus.

Wash them well, scrape, and tie them up in small bundles; cut them all even at the bottom, and as they are done put them into cold water; put them on in boiling water, with a little salt, and let them boil twenty or twenty-five minutes; take them up, lay them upon a slice of toasted bread cut in four, and the crusts pared off, with the tops meeting in the middle of the dish, and cut off the strings.

181.—Asparagus a la Francais.

Boil it, and chop small the heads and tender parts of the stalks, together with a boiled onion; add a little salt and pepper, and the beaten yolk of an egg; heat it up. Serve it on sippets of toasted bread, and pour over it a little melted butter.

182.—To Boil Brocoli.

Wash it, cut off all the outside leaves and stalks, throw it into cold water as it is trimmed, put it on in boiling water with a little salt, and boil it for twenty-five minutes or half an hour. It is sometimes served upon bits of toasted bread, and a little melted butter poured round it.

183.—To Boil Artichokes.

Cut off the stalks close to the bottom, wash them well, and let them lie for some hours in cold water; put them on in boiling water with a little salt in it, cover the pan closely, and boil them an hour and a half. If they are old, and have not been freshly gathered, they will take a longer time to boil. Melted butter is served with them in a sauce-tureen.

184.—To Boil Young Green Cabbages.

Wash and clean them well, put them on in boiling water with a little salt in it, and let them boil quickly from three-quarters to nearly an hour. Serve with melted butter.

185.—To Stew Cucumbers.

Pare eight or ten large cucumbers, and cut them into thick slices; flour them well, and fry them in butter; then put them into a saucepan with a teacupful of gravy; season it highly with cayenne, salt, mushroom catsup, and a little port wine. Let them stew for an hour, and serve them hot.

186.—*Another Way.*

Pare the cucumbers, and let them lie in vinegar and water with a little salt in it; drain them, and put them into a saucepan with a pint of gravy, a slice of lean ham, an onion stuck with one or two cloves, and a bunch of parsley and thyme; let them stew, closely covered, till tender. Take out the cucumbers, strain and thicken the gravy with a piece of butter rolled in flour, boil it up, and pour it over the cucumbers.

187.—To Stew Mushrooms.

Clean them as for pickling, and, after washing them, put them into a saucepan, with an anchovy, two cloves, some nutmeg sliced, mace, whole pepper, and salt; let them stew in their own liquor till tender.

In this way they will keep for some time, and when required to be dressed, pick out the spice, and to a dishful put two large tablespoonfuls of white wine; add part of their own liquor, and let them just boil; then stir in a bit of butter dredged with flour, and two tablespoonfuls of cream.

188.—*Another Way.*

For a good-sized dishful, take a pint of white stock; season it with salt, pepper, and a little lemon pickle; thicken it with a bit of butter rolled in flour; cleanse and peel the mushrooms, sprinkle them with a very little salt, boil them for three or four minutes, put them into the gravy when it is hot, and stew them for fifteen minutes.

189.—To Roast Onions.

Roast them with the skins on in an oven, that they may brown equally. They are eaten with cold fresh butter, pepper, and salt.

190.—Onions, Plain Boiled.

Peel them, and let them lie an hour in cold water, put them on in boiling milk and water; boil them till tender, and serve with melted butter poured over them.

191.—To Boil Carrots.

Scrape, wash, and clean them; put them on in boiling water with some salt in it, and boil them from two to three hours. Very young carrots will require one hour.

192.—Carrots, Flemish Way.

Prepare (after boiling) in the form of dice, balls, stars, crescents, &c., and stew with chopped parsley, young onions, salt and pepper, in plain melted butter, or good brown gravy.

193.—Green Peas Stewed.

Put a quart of good peas into a stewpan, with a lettuce and small onion sliced small, but not any water; add a piece of butter the size of an orange, pepper and salt to taste, and stew gently for two hours. Beat up an egg, and stir into them (or a lump of butter will do as well); mint should be stewed (if it can be procured) with them, and ought to be chopped fine, and stirred in with some good gravy.

194.—To Boil Green Peas.

After being shelled, wash them, drain them in a colander, put them on in plenty of boiling water, with a teaspoonful of salt, and one of pounded loaf sugar; boil them till they become tender, which, if young, will be in less than half an hour; if old, they will require more than an hour; drain them in a colander, and put them immediately into a dish with a slice of fresh butter in it. Some people think it an improvement to boil a small bunch of mint with the peas; it is then minced finely, and laid in small heaps at the end or sides of the dish. If peas are allowed to stand in the water after being boiled they lose their colour.

195.—To Stew Young Peas and Lettuce.

Wash and make perfectly clean one or two heads of cabbage lettuce, pick off the outside leaves, and lay them for two hours in cold water with a little salt in it; then slice them, and put them them into a saucepan, with a quart or three pints of peas, three tablespoonfuls of gravy, a bit of butter dredged with flower, some pepper and salt, and a teaspoonful of pounded loaf sugar. Let them stew, closely covered, till the peas are soft.

196.—Peas for a Second-course Dish, a la Francais.

Put a quart of fine green peas, together with a bit of butter the size of a walnut, into as much warm water as will cover them, in which let them stand for eight or ten minutes. Strain off the water, put them into a saucepan, cover it, stir them frequently, and when a little tender add a bunch of parsley and a young onion, nearly a dessertspoonful of loaf sugar, and an ounce of butter mixed with a teaspoonful of flour; keep stirring them now and then till the peas be tender, and add, if they become too thick, a tablespoonful of hot water. Before serving, take out the onion and bunch of parsley.

197.—To Steam Peas.

Shell and close-pack the peas securely in a large quantity of lettuce-salad leaves; put the package into a stewpan over a moderate fire for the ordinary time required to boil peas, say half an hour, when they will be ready.

198.—Vegetable Mash.

Take boiled potatoes, cauliflower, carrots, turnips, and green peas; mash down the potatoes with plenty of butter, pepper, and salt; mince small the cauliflower, carrots, and turnips, and add them with the peas to the mashed potatoes; mix them all well together, and serve up hot.

PASTRY, PUDDINGS, SWEETMEATS, ETC.

199.—Pastry for Pies and Tarts.

To every three ounces of flour take one ounce of soojee, two ounces of beef suet, and a little salt; pick and clean the suet, pound it in a mortar, and make a flat circular cake of it; make a dough of the flour and soojee, knead it well, divide it into two equal parts, and make them into two flat circular cakes quite as large as the suet cake; roll the three together, placing the suet cake between the two flour cakes; double the whole up twice, and roll it out again, when it will be ready for use.

200.—Pastry for Friar Tuck's Mock Venison Pasty Pie.

Take of veal one pound, and of udder one pound; pick, clean, and wash them; chop, mince, and pound them in a mortar; season with salt and white pepper; fix the mixture with the yolk and white of an egg well beaten up; pass it through a sieve, rejecting all that will not pass; and form it into a flat circular cake.

Make a dough of two pounds and a half of flour and half a pound of soojee; add a little salt, and knead it well; then form two cakes of the dough; place the veal and udder cake between, and roll out the three very carefully; double up the whole and roll it out again, when it will be ready.

The pie-dish should be lined thickly with the pastry, and, although a single layer should cover the top of the pie, the sides and edges of the dish should be built up high with it; a double layer of the crust is not interdicted to cover the top of the pie if it will not interfere with raising it up.

201.—Custard.

Take a seer of milk and a stick of cinnamon, and boil down to half the quantity; add sugar to taste; beat up quickly the yolks of four eggs, and add them gradually to the milk, stirring it continually; after a while thicken with a tablespoonful of rice flour; take it off the fire, and flavour with rose water, orange-flower water, or vanilla.

202.—Orange Custard.

Boil very tender the rind of half an orange, and beat it in a mortar until it is very fine; put to it a spoonful of the best brandy, the juice of an orange, four ounces of loaf sugar, and the yolk of four eggs; beat them altogether for ten minutes, and then pour in by degrees a pint of boiling milk; beat them until cold; then put them in custard-cups into a dish of hot water; let them stand till they are set; then take them out, and stick preserved orange-peel on the top. This forms a fine-flavoured dish, and may be served up hot or cold.

203.—Chocolate Custard.

Rasp three ounces of fine Spanish chocolate, which has the vanilla flavour; make a paste of it with the smallest possible quantity of water; put two pints of pure milk over the fire, and let it boil; then add powdered loaf sugar to your taste, and a *little* salt; meanwhile, beat up the chocolate with some of the milk as it boils, and mix it well; pour it into the boiling milk, which you must keep in motion; add the yolks of eight eggs well beaten up; keep stirring in, or rather milling the mixture, until of sufficient consistency; when cool enough put the custards into glasses.

204.—Almond Custard.

Blanch and pound, with two tablespoonfuls of orange-flower water, a quarter of a pound of almonds; add rather more than a pint of milk, thickened with a teaspoonful of corn-flour, and the well-beaten-up yolks of six eggs; sweeten to taste with pounded loaf sugar, and stir it over a slow fire till it thickens, but do not allow it to boil. Serve up in glass custard-cups.

205.—Princess Royal Custard.

Beat up in a large deep bowl the yolks of eight fresh eggs; dredge into it while beating up a dessertspoonful of corn-flour; sweeten to taste with the best pounded loaf sugar; add to it a quarter of a pound of Jordan almonds well bruised in a marble mortar; pour the mixture into a clean newly-tinned copper pan; stir into it a seer of good cold milk; have a brisk flaming fire ready. Put the pan on the fire; never cease stirring it, keeping the spoon as much as possible in the centre of the pan; reduce the flame after it has boiled for fifteen minutes, and continue to boil for a few minutes longer, until the custard is of the consistency required.

Fill the custard cups or glasses, leaving about half an inch space to fill up with the whites of the eggs, beaten up to a very light froth, which should be done a quarter or half an hour before serving up. While it is being beaten up, flavour it with a little essence of almonds, or orange-flower water.

206.—Rose-bloom Custard.

This is made in every respect like the foregoing, adding some bruised almonds, and a little rose-bloom to tint the custard. The froth of the white of the eggs is also tinted with a few drops of the rose-bloom.

207.—Blanc Mange.

Boil, till dissolved, three-fourths of an ounce of isinglass in as much water as will cover it; when lukewarm, add to it gradually a quart of good rich milk, with a stick of cinnamon, some lemon-peel, and a few bitter almonds well pounded; sweeten to taste; boil for five or six minutes, stirring it all the while; strain through muslin into moulds, and place in a pan of cold water to congeal.

208.—*Another Way.*

Blanch and pound with a little rose-water two ounces of sweet and six bitter almonds; dissolve three-fourths of an ounce of isinglass in a little water; when nearly cool, mix it into a quart of good rich milk; mix in the almonds the peel of a small lemon and a stick of cinnamon; sweeten to taste with good clean sugar; let it stand for two or three hours; then put it into a pan, and let it boil for six or eight minutes, stirring it constantly; strain through muslin, and keep stirring it until nearly cold; then pour it into moulds.

209.—Rice Blanc Mange.

Mix to a stiff smooth paste four tablespoonfuls of finely-sifted ground rice-flour, with a little cold milk; then stir it into a quart of boiling milk, in which had been dissolved one-eighth of an ounce of isinglass, a stick of cinnamon, and the peel of half a small lemon; sweeten to taste; boil it from ten to fifteen minutes, stirring it carefully all the while; remove it from the fire, and mix into it briskly a tablespoonful of pounded almonds, and pour it while scalding hot into moulds previously dipped in *cold* water.

N.B.—If it be desired to tint it in streaks like marble, drop into the mould every here and there, at the time of pouring the blanc mange, some of the cochineal, recipe No. 268.

210.—Corn-flour Blanc Mange.

The above recipe will answer, except that the quantity of corn-flour must be in the proportion of two tablespoonfuls to every quart of milk.

211.—Christmas Plum Pudding (Indian Way).

This pudding may be made a few days before it is required for the table.

Take of cleaned and picked raisins one pound and a half, currants half a pound, finely-grated bread-crumbs three-quarters of a pound, finely-sliced mixed peel half a pound, finely-minced suet three-quarters of a pound, and sugar three-quarters of a pound. Mix all these well together with half a teaspoonful of finely-powdered mixed spices, say cinnamon, nutmeg, and mace; then moisten the mixture with half a pound of butter free of water, twelve eggs well beaten, and a wineglassful of brandy, stirring it well the whole time, that the ingredients may be thoroughly mixed.

Butter a large piece of cloth or napkin; dredge it well with flour; put the mixture into it, and tie it down tightly; after boiling it steadily for seven hours take it out of the boiler and hang it up immediately, until the day it is intended to be eaten, when it should be boiled again for fully two hours, care being taken that the water is boiling before the pudding is put into it. Then turn it out of the towel, and serve up with brandy sauce.

212.—Bombay Pudding.

Take two pounds or one seer of soojee, half roast it, then boil it in water until it becomes very thick; butter a soup-plate or any other dish of about the same depth; pour the boiled soojee into it; when it has cooled and congealed, cut it into eight or more cakes; rub the cakes over with the yolk of an egg, dredge with finely-sifted flour, and fry in ghee until they acquire a rich brown colour. Arrange them in a dish, and pour over them a thick syrup flavoured with lemon-juice.

213.—*Another Way.*

Make a good sweet custard and set it aside; rasp fine a cocoanut, and fry it in a little butter with grated nutmeg; pour into it gradually a wineglassful of brandy, stirring it all the time; have a pudding-dish lined with a good puff paste; pour the fried cocoanut gradually into the custard, stirring it well all the while; fill the pudding-dish with the mixture, and bake it in a gentle oven for fifteen to twenty minutes, or until the pudding is cooked.

214.—Cocoanut Rice Pudding.

Soak a breakfastcupful of fine rice in water until quite soft; scoop out the contents of a hard cocoanut; extract all the milk with a little boiling-hot water, then boil the rice in it, sweeten it to taste with some date jagree or treacle, and put in a few grains of aniseed. Pour the mixture into a buttered pudding-dish and bake it slightly.

215.—Indian Lemon Pudding.

Take four chittacks or eight ounces of butter free of water, six chittacks or twelve ounces of white sugar, twelve fresh eggs, four wineglassfuls of lemon or lime juice, and four tablespoonfuls of finely-grated bread-crumbs. Mix the butter and the sugar, add the yolks of the eggs, then the lime-juice and bread-crumbs, and when the oven is ready add the whites of the eggs well beaten up, put the whole into a buttered pudding-dish, and bake it immediately.

216.—Marmalade Pudding.

This pudding requires care in mixing the ingredients thoroughly together, but it proves so excellent when eaten, either cold or hot, that it fully repays the trouble of preparation. Shred six ounces of fresh beef suet, and chop it up fine; mix it with two ounces of moist sugar, a quarter of a pound of well-grated bread-crumbs, and then stir in half a pint of new milk; when these are all mixed, add the well-beaten yolks of three eggs, whisk all together for a quarter of an hour, and set it to stand on a cold stone for an hour. Butter a pudding-dish or mould thickly, place a layer of the above mixture in it, then a layer of marmalade, another layer of mixture, and so on alternately until the mixture is exhausted. For the above quantity about one pound of marmalade will be required. Whisk the whites of the eggs with a little loaf sugar and orange-flower water, place the froth at the top of the pudding, and bake for an hour and a half in a moderate oven.

217.—Custard Pudding.

Mix with a pint of cream or milk six well-beaten eggs, two tablespoonfuls of finely-sifted flour, half a small nutmeg grated, or an equal quantity of pounded cinnamon, a tablespoonful of pounded loaf sugar, and a little salt; put it into a cloth or buttered basin, that will exactly hold it, and boil it for half an hour. Serve with wine sauce.

218.—Macaroni.

Take the yolks and white of two fresh eggs, and as much finely-sifted flour (English or American preferable to country) as will make a good dough of the consistency of dough for pie-crusts without the addition of any water; roll it out to its full extent on a large board to about the thickness of an eight-anna piece; then cut it up into small squares, diamonds, or circles, or into any shape or design you please, which must be done quickly, as within an hour of its being rolled out the pastry will harden. It may be used immediately, or in the winter it may be kept good for a few days.

N.B.—If pipe macaroni be required, cut the macaroni in ribbons of the required width, dredge some flour over it, and put it lengthways over glass pipes, joining the two cut ends with the aid of a little raw egg, and draw the pipes out as the pastry hardens round them. For pipe macaroni, the pastry should be rolled finer.

219.—Tart and Pie Crusts of Soojee.

To one seer and a quarter of soojee add half a seer of suet and a teaspoonful of salt. Thoroughly clean the suet, remove all the skin and other obectionable particles, chop, mince, and pound fine in a mortar. Damp the soojee for half an hour before kneading it, then knead it with the suet and a little of the yeast, recipe No. 283; divide it into parts, dredge it with flour, and roll in layers; repeat the operation two or three times, and the pastry when baked will be light and flaky. Half a seer of flour will be required for dredging and rolling.

Chappatee or Hand-bread.

The native hand-bread is made simply of wheat-flour and water; the addition of a little salt would be an improvement. Make a good dough of flour and water, take a piece about the size of an egg, roll it out to the circumference of a half-plate, and bake it over an iron or earthen plate.

221.—Dalpooree.

Prepare a dal chur churree, recipe No. 93; put it into a marble mortar, and reduce it to a fine paste. Prepare an ordinary pie pastry; take two pieces of the prepared dough, each of the size of a walnut; shape them into two small bowls; take as much of the dal paste as will make a ball of the size of a walnut; put it into one of the bowls of dough, and cover it over with the other bowl, and then roll out the whole very carefully to the size of a dinner-plate, and fry in ghee of a very light yellow colour. The lighter and thinner dalpoorees can be made the better. They should be eaten hot.

222.—Dal Pittas.

Prepare an ordinary pie-crust, and the dal chur churree, recipe No. 93; roll out the pastry, cut into circles of the size of saucers, put into them a tablespoonful of the dal, and close them; fry in ghee of a light brown colour. They should be eaten hot.

223.—Prawn Doopiaja Pittas.

The same as the above, enclosing in the pastry a tablespoonful of the prawn doopiaja, recipe No. 69; fry in ghee.

N.B.—The prawns should be minced before being put into the pastry.

224.—Prawn Doopiaja Loaf.

Pare away very finely all the outer brown crust of the bread, without injuring the inner crust; cut out of the top of the loaf a small square sufficiently large to extract from within all the crumb, leaving the shell complete; then fill the loaf up to the top either with some prawn doopiaja minced, or with the prawn cofta curry, No. 37, and as much gravy as it will take; replace the square bit at the top, bake it to a light brown, and serve up hot.

225.—Fowl Doopiaja Loaf

Is made in the same way as the prawn loaf, the difference being that the shell of the bread is stuffed with either a fowl doopiaja, recipe No. 23, or with the chicken cofta curry, recipe No. 34; all the bones of the fowl will require to be removed before the bread is stuffed with the curry.

226.—Falooree.

Take of the finely-sifted flour of the chunna ka dal, which has been previously parched, one seer; six large Patna onions finely sliced and chopped; eight fresh green chilies sliced very fine; a tablespoonful each of finely-chopped soa mattee, saug, and parsley; a dessertspoonful of salt and a teaspoonful of finely-ground green ginger. Put the seer of dal-flour into a large deep pan, and mix into it all the above condiments; then keep adding to it water, very gradually and in small quantities at a time, mixing it briskly the whole while, until it is of a consistency that if poured on a plate from a spoon it will incline to a pyramid, or if dropped into a glass of water will not readily dissolve, but drop to the bottom *en masse*. In this state the mixture will be ready to fry.

Take half a seer of the best mustard oil; put it into a deep frying-pan with some fine slices of lemon-peel, and fry it or cook it thoroughly; remove three-fourths of the cooked oil from the frying-pan, and into the remainder, while boiling and bubbling, with a tablespoon pour in the preparation in the shape of rocks, and allow to brown, turning them over so that top and bottom may be of the same colour. As the oil is being expended clear the pan of all particles which may accumulate, pour in some more of the ready-cooked oil, and continue to fry until all the mixture is fried. They should be eaten hot.

227.—Cocoanut Pittas.

Scrape finely a cocoanut, brown it with some jagree and a few grains of the black cardamom seed, and set aside; then prepare a pastry of finely-sifted rice-flour (it must be kneaded with boiling-hot water, and will not roll out); take as much as the size of a duck's egg, and press it out flat in the palm of your hand to the size of a large saucer; put a tablespoonful of the fried cocoanut into it, and close it up in a half-moon shape, with the help of a little water. Have a wide-mouthed large earthen pot of boiling water; stretch and tie over its mouth a napkin, and steam the pittas or cakes over them; they will be ready in half an hour, and may be eaten hot or cold.

228.—Plantain Fritters.

Prepare a batter of twelve ripe plantains, four tablespoonfuls of finely-sifted flour, half a cupful of milk, sugar to taste, and cardamom and caraway seeds, with a couple of eggs beaten up; mix the whole well together, and make into small cakes by pouring a tablespoonful at a time of the mixture into melted ghee; fry them on both sides to a good brown colour, and serve up hot.

229.—Fried Plantains.

Slice or divide very ripe plantains lengthways into two; brush them slightly with the yolk of an egg; dredge with flour, and fry in melted ghee. Serve up hot, sprinkled with crushed crystallized sugar.

230.—Bibinca Dosee, or Portuguese Cocoanut Pudding.

Extract a cupful of milk from two cocoanuts, and set it aside. Make a syrup of three-quarters of a pound of sugar; mix into the syrup half a pound of rice-flour finely sifted, and the cocoanut milk, which boil over a good fire, stirring the whole while until it thickens; pour it into a buttered pudding-dish, and bake it of a rich light-brown colour.

231.—Bole Comadree, or Portuguese Cocoanut Pudding with Jagree.

Extract a cupful of milk from two cocoanuts, and set it aside. Make a syrup of half a pound of sugar; mix into it half a pound of finely-sifted rice-flour, and set aside; fry with the yolk of an egg all the scrapings of the two cocoanuts, half a pound of jagree, and some grains of aniseed; then mix the whole thoroughly together, and after the oven is well heated, and ready to receive the pudding, pour the mixture into a well-buttered pudding-dish, and bake over a slow fire until it is perfectly set.

232.—Goolgoola, or Fritters.

Take half a seer or one pound each of flour, sugar, and milk, half a dozen small sticks of cinnamon, a little yeast, and half a seer of ghee; mix the flour with the yeast and a little milk; add water sufficient to bring it to a thick consistency; then put into it gradually the sugar and the remainder of the milk, and place it on the fire, adding the cinnamon; keep stirring it with a large spoon until it is again reduced to a thick consistency; remove it from the fire, and when it has cooled make it up into small balls, and fry them in ghee.

233.—*Another Way (as usually served on the tea-table).*

Take two chittacks or four ounces of soojee, four eggs well beaten up and four chittacks or eight ounces of milk; mix the soojee and eggs, beating them well together, and gradually add the milk. Melt down three chittacks or six ounces of ghee in a small but deep pan; pour into the boiling ghee in one spot the mixture, a dessertspoonful at a time, and fry until of a rich brown colour. Serve up hot, sprinkled with crushed crystallized sugar.

234.—Cajure.

Mix one seer of soojee with four tablespoonfuls of ghee; add half a seer of sugar; mix well together; then pour in gradually a quarter of a seer of milk, and last of all as much flour as will make a good dough; let it be well kneaded, and then allowed to stand for two or three hours.

Have some ghee melted; take the dough of the size of walnuts, shape them like shells and fry them in the melted ghee until they acquire a rich brown colour.

235.—Hulluah.

Steep half a seer of soojee in one seer of water for twelve hours, or, if the hulluah be made in the winter, let it soak for eighteen hours; it will then be the "milk of soojee," which strain through a coarse duster, rejecting only such impurities as remain unstrained; add to the milk half a seer of sugar, and boil it, stirring it all the time, and as it thickens add three chittacks or six ounces of ghee, warmed with a few white cardamoms and a few small sticks of cinnamon; continue stirring it from first to last until the whole is well mixed together, and the hulluah finally taken out of the pan; while warm put it into shapes or moulds.

236.—*Another Way.*

Take half a seer each of soojee, ghee, sugar, almonds, and raisins, and a few white cardamoms and sticks of cinnamon. Make a syrup of the sugar, and set it aside. Roast the soojee, or brown it, and set it aside. Melt the ghee, and fry the soojee with the spices in it, after which put in the almonds and raisins, stirring it well all the time; last of all add the syrup, and continue to cook and stir it until it thickens; then remove into moulds or shapes while hot.

237.—A Two-pound or One-seer Plum Cake.

This is the favourite cake for Christmas, weddings, birthdays, and christenings in India, and consists of the following ingredients:—

Butter, perfectly free of water		4 lb. or 2 seers.
Good clean sugar		2 „ or 1 „
Raisins, cleaned, stoned, and dried		2 „ or 1 „
Currants, cleaned, stoned, picked, and dried		2 „ or 1 „
Jordan almonds, blanched and sliced very fine		2 „ or 1 „
Preserved ginger „ citron „ orange-peel „ lemon-peel „ pumpkin	All cut into small pieces and well dried, mixed	2 „ or 1 „
Cinnamon, finely pounded and sifted		1 Tablespoonful.
Nutmegs, finely grated		½ „
Dried orange-peel, finely pounded and sifted		½ „
English caraway-seeds, cleaned and picked		2 „
Mace, finely pounded and sifted		½ „
Finely-sifted flour		1½ lb. or ¾ seer.
Soojee		½ lb. or ¼ seer.
Eggs, new or fresh laid		40
Brandy of the best quality		1 claret-glass.

An experienced man ought to be engaged to mix the ingredients, which, if properly done, will take fully one hour.

Have two large glazed earthen preserving-pans; put the sugar into one, and bruise it well down, breaking all the lumps; add to it three pounds and three-quarters of butter; then throw in one by one all the yolks of the forty eggs, and throw the whites into the other preserving-pan, mixing the sugar, butter, and the yolks the whole while briskly and without ceasing. While one man is mixing these ingredients another ought to be actively employed in beating up the whites of the eggs unceasingly for nearly an hour.

After the butter has been well mixed with the sugar and eggs, dredge in all the finely-pounded spices and the caraway-seeds; after a while dredge in the flour and soojee in small quantities at a time (this must be well mixed); the currants, raisins, and preserves, with the almonds, are next to be added. By this time the man will have been engaged in mixing the ingredients fully three-quarters of an hour.

After the raisins, &c., have been thoroughly mixed, pour in the brandy very gradually, and in small quantities at a time, and last of all add the well-beaten whites of the forty eggs: the stirring now must be very brisk to effect a perfect mixture of the whites of the eggs right through; fill quickly into the moulds, and bake without a moment's delay in a brisk baker's oven.

N.B.—The moulds ought to be lined with paper and well buttered.

238.—Swiss Cakes.

Take butter, flour, and sugar, of each the weight of four eggs; beat the yolks with the sugar and some grated lemon-peel, or ten drops of essence of lemon, and one large teaspoonful of rose-water, or orange-flower water if preferred; add the butter just melted, and slowly shake in the flour, beating it until well mixed; beat the whites of the eggs to a froth, mix the whole together, and beat on for a few minutes after the whites are added. Butter a tin, and bake the cake half an hour.

239.—Queen Cakes.

Prepare eight ounces of fresh butter beaten to a cream, six ounces of pounded and sifted loaf sugar, half a pound of dried and sifted flour, the same quantity of cleaned and dried currants, four well-beaten eggs, a little grated nutmeg and pounded cinnamon, and a few pounded bitter almonds; then add the sugar to the butter, put in the eggs by degrees, after that the flour and the other ingredients; beat all well together for half an hour, and put it into small buttered tins, nearly filling them, and strew over the top finely-powdered loaf sugar. Bake them in a pretty brisk oven.

240.—Shrewsbury Cakes.

Mix with half a pound of fresh butter, washed in rose-water and beaten to a cream, the same quantity of dried and sifted flour, seven ounces of pounded and sifted loaf sugar, half an ounce of caraway-seeds, and two well-beaten eggs; make them into a paste, roll it thin, cut it into round cakes, prick them, and bake them upon floured tins.

241.—*Another Way.*

Rub into a pound of dried and sifted flour half a pound of fresh butter, seven ounces of sifted loaf sugar, the same quantity of cleaned and dried currants, and a little grated nutmeg; make it into a paste with a little water and two tablespoonfuls of rose or orange-flower water; roll it out, and cut it into round cakes; prick them, and bake them upon tins dusted with flour.

242.—Shortbread.

For two pounds of sifted flour, allow one pound of butter, a quarter of a pound of candied orange and lemon peel, a quarter of a pound each of pounded loaf sugar, blanched sweet almonds, and caraway comfits; cut the lemon, the orange-peel, and almonds into small thin bits, and mix them with a pound and a half of the flour, a few of the caraway comfits, and the sugar; melt the butter, and when cool, pour it into the flour, at the same time mixing it quickly with the hands; form it into a large round nearly an inch thick, using the remainder of the flour to make it up with; cut it into four, and with the finger and thumb pinch each bit neatly all round the edge; prick them with a fork, and strew the rest of the caraway comfits over the top. Put the pieces upon white paper dusted with flour, and then upon tins. Bake them in a moderate oven.

243.—Scotch Shortbread.

Warm before the fire two pounds of flour and one pound of butter free of water; rub the butter, with twelve ounces of sugar, into the flour with the hand and make it into a stiff paste with four eggs, well beaten: the rolling-out to the required thickness must be done with as little use of the rolling-pin as possible; either take small pieces, and roll them into oblong cakes, or roll out a large piece and cut it into squares or rounds; prick a pattern round the edge of each cake with the back of a knife, and arrange slices of candied peel, caraway-seeds, and caraway comfits in a pattern. They will take about twenty minutes to bake, and the oven should not be too quick. The mixing of flour, sugar, and butter, and afterwards of the eggs, must be done very thoroughly and smoothly.

244.—*Another Way.*

Take two pounds of flour, one pound of butter, four eggs, and twelve ounces of loaf sugar powdered very finely; rub the butter and sugar into the flour with the hand, and by means of the eggs convert it into a stiff paste; roll it out half an inch thick, and cut into square or round cakes; pinch up the edges to the height of about an inch, and on the top of each cake place some slices of candied peel and some large caraway comfits, pressed down so as to imbed about half of each in the cake. Bake in a warm oven upon iron plates.

245.—Gingerbread Nuts.

Take three pounds of flour, a pound of sugar, three pounds and a half of treacle, half an ounce of caraway-seeds, half an ounce of allspice, two ounces of butter, half an ounce of candied lemon-peel, three ounces of ground ginger, half an ounce of coriander, the yolks of three eggs, and a wineglassful of brandy; work the butter to a cream, then the eggs, spice, and brandy, then flour, sugar, and then hot treacle; if not stiff enough, a little more flour must be added in rolling out, but the less the better.

246.—*Another Way.*

Take two pounds of flour, one pound and a quarter of treacle, half a pound of sugar, two ounces of ginger, three-quarters of a pound of butter (melted), and a small quantity of cayenne pepper; mix all together and roll out to about the thickness of half an inch, or not quite so much; cut into cakes, and bake in a moderate oven.

247.—Ginger Cakes.

In two pounds of flour well mix three-quarters of a pound of good moist sugar and one ounce of the best Jamaica ginger; have ready three-quarters of a pound of lard melted, and four eggs well beaten; mix the lard and eggs together and stir into the flour, which will form a paste; roll out in thin cakes and bake in a moderately heated oven.

Lemon biscuits may be made the same way, substituting essence of lemon instead of ginger.

248.—Gingerbread Spiced.

Take three-quarters of a pound of treacle, one egg, four ounces of moist sugar, an ounce of powdered ginger, a quarter of an ounce each of mace, cloves, allspice, and nutmeg powdered, a pound of oiled butter, and sufficient flour to make a stiff paste; mix well, and make into thick pieces, which should be brushed over the top with white of egg and baked for an hour in a moderate oven.

249.—American Gingerbread.

Take half a pound of fresh butter melted, a pound and a half of dried and sifted flour, the same quantity of brown sugar, a quarter of a pound of pounded ginger, nine eggs, the yolks and whites separately beaten, one glass of rose-water, and one of white wine; mix all well together, and beat for an hour; then with a spoon spread it over flat tin pans, about the thickness of a penny-piece; bake it of a light brown, and while warm cut it into oblong pieces, and place them on end till cool, when they will be very crisp.

250.—Rich Gingerbread Cakes.

To one pound of dried and sifted flour allow half a pound of pounded loaf sugar, three-quarters of a pound of fresh butter washed in rose-water, one pound of treacle, one nutmeg grated, the weight of a nutmeg of pounded mace, and as much of pounded cinnamon, one ounce of pounded ginger, one and a half of candied orange and lemon peel cut small, half an ounce of blanched sweet almonds cut into long thin bits, and two well-beaten eggs. Melt the butter with the treacle, and when nearly cold stir in the eggs and the rest of the ingredients; mix all well together, make it into round cakes, and bake them upon tins.

251.—Indian Gingerbread.

Take twelve ounces of pounded loaf sugar, a quarter of a pound of fresh butter, one pound of dried flour, two ounces of pounded ginger, and a quarter of an ounce each of cloves and cinnamon. Mix the ginger and the spice with the flour; put the sugar and a small teacupful of water into a saucepan; when it is dissolved add the butter, and as soon as it is melted mix it with the flour and other things; work it up, form the paste into cakes or nuts, and bake them upon tins.

252.—Oatmeal Gingerbread.

Gingerbread made with oatmeal instead of flour, besides being nice, is a very useful aperient for children.

253.—Excellent Cheesecakes, known at Richmond as "Maids of Honour."

Take half a pound of curd free of the whey; add to it six ounces of butter, four yolks of eggs, and sugar and nutmeg to the taste; mix all the ingredients well; line patty-pans with a puff paste, fill them with the mixture, and bake in a quick oven. The cheesecakes may be flavoured with lemon for a variety, and, as a further variety, currants and raisins may be introduced.

254.—Cocoanut Cheesecakes.

Grate a good-sized nut very fine, and add to it four or five spoonfuls of rich syrup and one spoonful of rose-water; set it over a few coals, and keep stirring till it is mixed; then take it off the fire and let it cool; next mix the yolks of two eggs well with it, and bake in small pans in the shape of cheesecakes. The pastry for the pans must be made with flour and yolks of eggs, rolled as thin as possible; wet the tops of the cakes with rose-water; sift some refined sugar over them, and bake them in an oven at a gentle heat.

255.—Buns.

Mix together one pound of flour, six ounces of butter, two teaspoonfuls of baking powder, a quarter of a pound of sugar, one egg, nearly a quarter of a pint of milk, and a few drops of essence of lemon. Bake immediately. The above quantities will make twenty-four buns; for variety, currants or raisins may be added.

256.—Rout Cakes.

To one pound of ground almonds add one pound of powdered sugar; mix them together with yolks of eggs to a stiff, yet flexible paste; then form it into small biscuits in the shape of coronets, shells, filberts, birds' nests, rings, or any other fancy shapes; let them remain five or six hours, or all night, upon the baking-tin in a warm oven.

257.—French Pancakes.

Beat separately the yolks and whites of seven eggs; beat with the yolks four tablespoonfuls of pounded loaf sugar, the same quantity of flour, one pint of cream or milk, the grated peel and juice of one lemon, and two tablespoonfuls of rose-water; add the beaten whites the last thing. Allow three tablespoonfuls to each pancake.

258.—Common Pancakes.

With nearly half a pound of flour mix five well-beaten eggs, and then add, by degrees, a quart of good milk; fry them in fresh lard, and serve them with pounded loaf sugar strewed between each.

259.—Indian Pancakes.

Add to three well-beaten eggs a pint of new milk, three tablespoonfuls of flour, some sugar, and a little pounded cinnamon; mix all well together, and fry in butter; brown the upper side for a minute before the fire; serve it, cut into four, with pounded sugar strewed over it.

260.—Pink Pancakes.

These are rarely seen at an English table, although they form a very pleasing variety. Boil a large red beetroot until it is very tender; then peel it, cut it into thin slices, pound it to a pulp in a marble mortar, and strain through muslin; add the yolks of five eggs, two tablespoonfuls of flour, four of cream, plenty of pounded loaf sugar, half a nutmeg grated, and a wineglassful of brandy; rub the whole into a batter, and fry the pancakes with melted butter, ghee, or lard; serve them up hot, garnished with green candied sweetmeats.

261.—Mango Fool.

Take six green mangoes; remove every particle of the green peel, cut them into four, and steep them in clean water; throw the stones away; boil the fruit perfectly tender, pulp and pass it through a sieve, sweeten to your taste, and add to it very gradually, stirring all the while, as much good pure milk as will reduce it to the consistency of custard. It should be eaten on the day it is made.

262.—*Another Way.*

Boil to a pulp some green mangoes without peel or stones; pass through a sieve, and sweeten to taste; then mix into it very gradually some cold milk, which has been previously boiled; keep stirring until it has acquired the thickness of an ordinary cream custard; fill into glass cups, and grate a little cinnamon or nutmeg over them.

263.—Pink Mango Fool.

The pink mango fool is produced by the introduction of beetroot boiled very tender, bruised down, strained through muslin, and added to the pulp of the mango, and forms an agreeable variety.

264.—Vanilla Drops.

Take the whites of four eggs, beat them up well, and add three-quarters of a pound of finely-powdered white sugar; flavour with vanilla, beat up well, and drop it on buttered paper. Bake in a cool oven.

265.—Mincemeat.

Ingredients:—Three large lemons, three large apples, one pound of stoned raisins, one pound of currants, one pound of suet, two pounds of moist sugar, one pound of sliced candied orange-peel, one ounce of sliced candied citron, the same quantity of lemon-peel, one teacupful of brandy, and two tablespoonfuls of orange marmalade.

Grate the rinds of the lemons, squeeze out the juice, strain it, and boil the remainder of the lemons until tender enough to pulp or chop very finely; then add to this pulp the apples, which should be baked, and their skins and cores removed; put in the remaining ingredients one by one, and as they are added mix everything thoroughly together. Put the mincemeat into a stone jar with a closely-fitting lid, and in a fortnight it will be ready for use. This should be made the first or second week in December.

266.—*Another Way.*

Take seven pounds of currants well picked and cleaned; of finely-chopped beef suet, the lean of sirloin of beef minced raw, and citron, lemon, and orange peel cut small, each half a pound; two pounds of fine moist sugar, an ounce of mixed spice, and the rinds of four lemons and four oranges; mix well, and put in a deep pan. Mix a bottle of brandy and white wine and the juice of the four lemons and oranges; pour half over, and press down tight with the hand; then add the other half and cover closely. It may be made one year, to use the next.

267.—Ornament for Custards or Creams.

Whisk for an hour the whites of two eggs, together with two tablespoonfuls of some syrup or thin jelly; lay it in any form upon a custard or cream, piled up to imitate rock, or it may be served in a dish with cream round it. The ornament may be coloured, if desired, with cochineal, saffron, spinach, &c., as directed in the following recipe.

268.—Colouring for Jellies, Creams, Ices, and Cakes.

Boil very slowly in a gill of water, till reduced to one half, twenty grains of cochineal, and the same quantity of alum and cream of tartar finely pounded; strain, and keep it in a small phial.

For yellow, use an infusion of saffron.

For green, wash well, and pull into small bits, a handful of spinach-leaves; put them into a closely-covered saucepan, let them boil for a few minutes, and then press the juice.

269.—Colouring Mixtures.

Yellow.—Into a four-ounce phial put half a drachm of saffron and two ounces of spirits of wine of the strength of sixty-two degrees over proof. Let it stand until the spirit is tinted of a deep yellow; then strain it for use.

Red.—This is produced by infusing during a fortnight two ounces of red sandal-wood in a pint of spirits of wine. If at the expiration of that time the colour should not be dark enough, a pinch of subcarbonate of soda will give it the required tint.

Pink.—Dissolve half an ounce of cochineal in a sufficient quantity of spirits of wine.

Green.—Put a handful of well-cleansed vine-leaves or spinach into a decanter, fill with spirits of wine, and let it stand in the sun for ten or twelve days; strain when the wine has become of a bright green.

N.B.—The above colouring matters are only adapted for tinting liqueurs, wines, lemonade, and essences.

270.—Frost or Icing for Cakes.

Beat till very light the whites of four eggs, and add gradually three-quarters of a pound of double-refined sugar, pounded and sifted through a lawn sieve; mix in the juice of half a lemon; beat it till very light and white; place the cake before the fire, pour over it the icing, and smooth over the top and sides with the back of a spoon.

271.—*Another Way.*

Beat to a stiff froth the whites of three new-laid eggs, and add to them one pound of sifted white sugar; flour the cake, and then wipe it off; apply the icing by means of a knife smoothly; then bake in a slow oven.

272.—Coloured Icings.

Pink icing should be made by adding cochineal syrup; blue, with indigo; yellow, with saffron or gamboge; green, with spinach syrup or sap green; brown, with chocolate.

273.—Fine Icing for Tarts and Puffs.

Pound and sift four ounces of refined loaf sugar; beat up the white of an egg, and by degrees add to it the sugar till it looks white and is thick. When the tarts are baked, lay the icing over the top with a brush or feather, and then return them to the oven to harden, but take care that they do not become brown.

274.—Raspberry Iced Cream.

Mix a tablespoonful of pounded loaf sugar, two tablespoonfuls of raspberry jelly or jam, and a little cochineal to heighten the colour, with the juice of a large lemon; strain, and put into the freezing-pot; cover it closely and place it in a bucket which has a small hole near the bottom, and a spigot to let the water run off, with plenty of ice broken small, and mixed with three or four handfuls of coarse salt; press the ice closely round the freezing-pot, turn it round and round for about ten minutes, take off the cover, and remove with a spoon the frozen cream to the centre; cover it again, and turn it till all be equally iced. Serve it in china ice-pails in block, or put it into moulds, cover them securely, and replace them in the bucket, with ice and salt as before, for an hour or more; dip the moulds into cold water before turning out, and serve immediately. Water ices are made in this way, substituting water for cream.

275.—Apricot Iced Cream.

Mix a tablespoonful of pounded loaf sugar with two of apricot jam, the juice of a lemon, and half an ounce of blanched bitter almonds pounded with a little rose-water; add a pint of cream, stir all well together before putting it into the freezing-pot, and freeze it as directed above.

276.—Mille Fruit Iced Cream.

Strain the juice of three lemons, and grate the peel of one; mince finely a dessertspoonful each of orange marmalade, dried cherries, and preserved angelica; add to these half a pint of syrup, and mix the whole with a pint and a half of cream, or a pint of water, and then drop in here and there a few drops of the prepared cochineal. Put it into a mould, and freeze as above directed.

277.—Orange-water Iced.

Mix with a pint of water the strained juice of three oranges and one lemon, also the grated peel of one orange; sweeten it well with syrup, and freeze it.

278.—Juice of Fruit Iced.

Press through a sieve the juice of a pint of currants or raspberries, or other fruit preserved for tarts; add to it four or five ounces of pounded loaf sugar, a little lemon-juice, and a pint of cream. It may be whisked previous to freezing, and a mixture of the juice in which the fruit was preserved may be used.

279.—Orange Iced Cream.

Boil down a seer and a half of milk to half the quantity with some isinglass and a quarter of a seer or half a pound of sugar; strain through a sieve, and when perfectly cool add the juice of twelve oranges. Mix well, put into freezing-pots with two seers or four pounds of raw rice and some salt, and freeze as above.

280.—Bael Sherbet.

Take a perfectly ripe sweet bael, and scoop out the whole contents into a bowl; make a paste of it with a little water; then add sugar to taste, and as much water as will bring it to the consistency of good honey; then pass it through a fine sieve, leaving all the fibres and seeds behind: it is a most delicious drink, and if taken early in the morning in rather a liquid state—say of the consistency of porter—serves as a most effective aperient in a natural and healthy form; but if taken of the consistency of thick pea or potato soup, it has a directly contrary effect, and as such is invaluable in all cases of relaxed bowels.

281.—Mallie, or Cream as prepared by the Natives.

Boil down over a slow fire milk to less than half its original quantity, and when cold it will be of the strength and consistency of a well-made blanc mange.

N.B.—The best Indian sweetmeats are made of mallie.

282.—Tyre or Dhye.

Warm some milk without boiling it; stir into it a little stale butter about the size of a large pea; put the vessel in a warm place well covered over, and in the course of eight or ten hours the tyre will be ready.

283.—Yeast.

Boil one pound of good flour, a quarter of a pound of brown sugar, and a little salt in two gallons of water for one hour; when milk-warm, bottle it close: it will be fit to use in twenty-four hours. One pint of this will make eighteen pounds of bread.

284.—*Another Way.*

Take two pounds of soojee or flour, a quarter of a pound of brown sugar or suckur, and half a drachm of hops. Dry the hops in the sun, and then reduce them to fine powder, by pounding in a mortar. Mix the soojee or flour and powdered hops with a little water, just sufficient to make a stiff dough; then add the sugar and knead all well together. Roll the leaven into a ball, wrap it lightly in a clean cloth, then in a blanket, and put it away for three days, when it will be ready for use.

N.B.—If worked up or kneaded once daily during the three days, the fermentation will be more perfect.

The above quantity will be sufficient for twenty-five pounds weight of bread.

GARNISHES, SAUCES, STUFFINGS, ETC.,

FOR FISH, ROAST AND BOILED MEATS, MADE DISHES, PUDDINGS, ETC.

285.—**Casserole of Potatoes.**

Peel and boil some good mealy potatoes, pound them, and mix with them some butter, cream, and a little salt; put them about an inch and a half high upon a dish, and leave an opening in the centre; bake it of a light brown colour, and take out as much more from the centre as will admit of a ragout, fricassee cutlet, or macaroni being put in.

286.—**Rissoles or Croquets.**

Mince very finely some cold roast meat or fowl and a small bit of bacon; season it with grated nutmeg and salt; moisten it with cream, and make it up into good-sized balls; dip them into yolks of eggs beaten up, and then into finely-grated bread. Bake them in an oven, or fry of a light brown colour. Before serving, drain them before a fire on the back of a sieve. Garnish with fried parsley.

287.—**Fricandellans.**

Mince about two pounds of tender lean beef and three-quarters of a pound of fresh suet; then pound till it is as smooth as a paste, and carefully pick out all the threads and sinews; add four well-beaten eggs, half a pint of rich cream, and as much grated and sifted bread as will make it sufficiently consistent to form into rolls resembling corks; and season with salt and pepper. Boil the corks in some good stock, or in boiling water, or fry them.

288.—Forcemeat.

Mince very finely the following ingredients:—Three ounces of fresh beef suet, one of fat bacon, three of raw or dressed veal, two of grated bread, a little grated lemon-peel, nutmeg, pepper, salt, and finely-minced parsley; mix all well together, and bind with the beaten yolks of eggs; make it into croquets or balls, the size of large nutmegs, and fry them in ghee or clarified beef dripping, or use it for stuffing.

289.—Forcemeat Balls

May be made of pounded veal or mutton, minced beef suet or fat of veal, taking an equal quantity of meat, suet, and grated bread-crumbs; add a bit of fat bacon chopped, season with salt, pepper, and grated nutmeg, and mix all well together with the beaten yolk of an egg.

290.—*Another Way.*

To half a pound of beef or veal add half a pound of udder; mince and pound to a pulp in a mortar; remove all gristle and parts not pulped, and mix with it the finely-grated crumbs of a slice of stale bread, and a tablespoonful of finely-chopped parsley; soften down the whole with some milk or gravy, then add a teaspoonful of finely-pounded pepper and a teaspoonful of salt; rub down the whole well together, and add the whites and yolks of two raw eggs, well beaten up; make into balls. If for soup, the size of the balls should be that of small nutmegs; if to garnish made dishes, make them into the size of large walnuts or of ordinary croquets or rissoles.

291.—Forcemeat Onions.

Peel four or five large onions, scoop out the inside, fill them with forcemeat, and roast them in an oven.

They may be served with roast turkey or fowl.

292.—Forcemeat for Fish.

Pick from the bones the meat of a large beckty, hilsa, or any sort of white fish; mince it finely, and add the same proportions of minced suet and grated bread, a few chopped oysters, and some boiled parsley chopped; season with a little pounded onion, cayenne pepper, salt, nutmeg, and lemon-peel; mix all well together, and bind it with the well-beaten yolks of eggs; roll it into small balls, and fry them.

293.—Egg Balls.

Grind down to a powder or paste the yolks of four hard-boiled eggs; add a teaspoonful of very finely sifted flour, some tender leaves of parsley, finely chopped, and a little white pepper and salt; grind, and mix all well together with the yolk of a raw egg; roll into small balls, and boil for two or three minutes.

294.—Brain Cakes.

Having previously boiled down the brains, bruise them, and add a teaspoonful of finely-sifted flour, some grated nutmeg, pepper, and salt, and a raw egg; then roll out like piecrust to the thickness of a rupee, punch out cakes of the size of Spanish dollars, and fry them.

295.—*Another Way.*

Take the brains and remove any veins, &c.; chop well with a knife, add salt, nutmeg, and pepper, a little raw egg, and flour enough to make them stick together; mix well, make into cakes about the size of the top of liqueur glasses, and fry them brown on both sides.

296.—Sauce for Salads.

Bruise down when quite cold the yolks of four hard-boiled eggs, and rub into them half a teaspoonful of pepper, one of salt and one tablespoonful of sugar, with two to three teaspoonfuls of prepared mustard. When well rubbed together, add very gradually four tablespoonfuls of oil, stirring it the whole while; when well mixed add a dessertspoonful of Lee and Perrin's Worcestershire sauce, one tablespoonful and a half of white wine vinegar, and a dessertspoonful of tarragon vinegar.

If the sauce be required thicker than usual, take either a larger number of eggs or a teaspoonful or a dessertspoonful of corn or other flour; put it into a cup, pour over it the quantity of vinegar prescribed above, place the cup in a saucepan of boiling water over the fire, and stir until the vinegar thickens to the desired consistency; then mix it gradually into the preparation of eggs, oil, &c.

297.—Sauce for Lobster Salad.

Observe all the directions given in the foregoing recipe, adding to the yolks of the hard-boiled eggs some of the spawn or red coral of the lobsters and a dash of essence of anchovy. Omit the sugar, and instead of the Worcestershire sauce substitute mushroom catsup and Indian tapp sauce.

298.—Excellent Fish Sauce.

Wash and bone two anchovies, and rub them up in a mortar with a quarter of a pound of butter and half a teaspoonful of flour. Put these into a small saucepan; then add to the yolks of three eggs well beaten up, two tablespoonfuls of tarragon vinegar, a small bunch of sweet herbs, consisting of parsley, green onions, and a bay-leaf, and a little salt, pepper, and nutmeg; stir these over the fire until the sauce is thick, but be careful not to let it boil, or it will burn. Serve it up in a sauce-tureen.

299.—Sauce for Boiled Mutton or Boiled Brisket or Beef.

Warm a saucepan, and melt in it two chittacks or four ounces of butter free of water; fry in it a tablespoonful of finely-sliced onions; when half browned, put in gradually two tablespoonfuls of finely-sifted flour, taking care to keep stirring it the whole time; then add gradually eight chittacks or sixteen ounces of pure milk, and lastly two wineglasses of vinegar, with finely-pounded white pepper and salt to taste. This sauce is without its equal.

300.—Fresh Tomato Gravy Sauce for Made Dishes.

Take forty tomatoes (halved), some soup herbs, and salt; boil them in a little stock; strain through a sieve, replace on the fire, and thicken with the addition, more or less, of a dessertspoonful of arrowroot or corn or other flour, to obtain any required consistency; finally add a teaspoonful of good English vinegar; if a sharper gravy sauce be desired, instead of the vinegar add either a dessertspoonful of tapp sauce or a teaspoonful of chili vinegar.

301.—Tapp Sauce Gravy for Made Dishes.

Thicken a good seasoned stock with arrowroot or corn-flour; add to every cup of the thickened stock a tablespoonful of tapp sauce. Pour it while hot over chicken, veal, beef, or prawn cutlets, or other made dishes.

302.—Sauce for Cucumber Salad.

Slice into a soup-plate two large Patna onions and a couple of fresh chilies; sprinkle over with ground pepper and a little salt; then add two tablespoonfuls of vinegar, and allow to stand for two or three hours before adding to it the sliced cucumbers. This sauce is also used occasionally for lobster and prawn salads.

303.—Parsley Sauce.

Pick, clean, and mince fine some fresh green crisp parsley, and put it into a tureen with a tablespoonful of chopped capers and a teaspoonful of good English vinegar. Fry to a nice light brown a dessertspoonful of curry onions in two chittacks or four ounces of butter, free of water; add a cup of good white stock, free of fat, and thicken with crumb of stale bread finely grated, a teaspoonful of salt, and a little pepper; allow to simmer until of a sufficient consistency; then pour it over the minced parsley and capers, mix well together, and it is ready for use.

304.—Onion Sauce.

Clean and boil six or eight good Patna onions; allow the water to drain away; fry to a light brown colour, in two chittacks or four ounces of butter, free of water, a dessertspoonful of finely-sliced curry onions; then gradually mix into it a tablespoonful of finely-sifted flour and half a seer of milk, taking care through the whole operation to keep stirring the sauce to prevent its lumping; add a teaspoonful of salt and a quarter of a teaspoonful of pepper; last of all add the boiled onions, and in a few minutes the sauce will be ready.

305.—White Onion Sauce.

Peel and cut in halves eight large and perfectly sound white Patna onions, and steep them in water for half an hour; then boil them until quite tender; drain them of all water; then chop and bruise them fine, and put them into a saucepan, with half a chittack or one ounce of butter, half a teaspoonful of salt, and some milk; put the mixture over a brisk fire, and keep stirring till it boils; then rub the whole through a sieve; after which add sufficient milk to make the sauce of the consistency required. This is a favourite sauce for boiled mutton, over which some occasionally strew a tablespoonful of capers.

306.—Brown Onion Sauce for Gravy.

Heat one chittack or two ounces of butter, free of water, in which fry to a light brown half a dozen well-selected white Patna onions finely sliced; then stir into it gradually half a chittack or one ounce of flour; add a little stock and some pepper and salt, boil up for a few minutes, strain through a sieve, and then add a tablespoonful of port wine, and the same of mushroom catsup. Lemon-juice or vinegar may be added if a sharper gravy be required.

307.—Sauce for Boiled Beef.

Mince a large onion, parboil it, and drain off the water; put the onion into a saucepan, with a tablespoonful of finely-chopped parsley, some good gravy, and one ounce of butter dredged with a little flour; let it boil nearly ten minutes, and add a spoonful of cut capers. The sauce must be thoroughly heated before being served up.

308.—Sauce for any kind of Meat.

Take three tablespoonfuls of gravy, two of vinegar, a blade of mace, a little pepper and salt, and a large onion sliced; boil and strain.

309.—Lobster Sauce.

Pound very finely the spawn of a lobster, rub it through a sieve, mix it with a quarter of a pound of melted butter, and then add the meat of the lobster cut into small bits. Make it quite hot, but do not allow it to boil.

310.—Oyster Sauce.

Beard and scald the oysters; strain the liquor, and thicken it with a little flour and butter; squeeze in a little lemon-juice, and add three tablespoonfuls of cream. Heat it well, but do not let it boil.

311.—Sauce for Roast Beef.

Mix well together a large tablespoonful of finely-grated horseradish, a dessertspoonful of made mustard, and half a dessertspoonful of brown sugar; then add vinegar till it be as thick as made mustard. Serve in a sauce-tureen.

312.—To make a Quart Bottle of Fish or Meat Sauce.

To half a bottle of vinegar put one ounce of cayenne, two cloves of garlic, one tablespoonful of soy, two of walnut, and two of mushroom catsup. Let it stand six days, shaking it frequently; then add the remaining half of the bottle of vinegar, let it stand another week, strain, and put it into small bottles.

313.—Pink Sauce for Fish.

Put into a pan, or wide-mouthed jar, one quart of good vinegar, half a pint of port wine, half an ounce of cayenne, one large tablespoonful of walnut catsup, two of anchovy liquor, a quarter of an ounce of cochineal, and six cloves of garlic. Let it remain forty hours, stirring it two or three times a day; run it through a flannel bag, and put it into half-pint bottles.

314.—Bread Sauce.

Boil in a pint of water the crumb of a French roll or of a slice of bread, a minced onion, and some whole pepper; when the onion is tender drain off the water, pick out the peppercorns, and rub the bread through a sieve; then put it into a saucepan, with a gill of cream, a bit of butter, and a little salt; stir it till it boils, and serve in a sauce-tureen.

315.—Apple Sauce.

Pare, core, and slice some apples; boil them in water with a bit of lemon-peel; when tender, mash them; add to them a bit of butter the size of a walnut, and some brown sugar. Heat, and serve in a sauce-tureen.

316.—Egg Sauce.

Boil three or four eggs about a quarter of an hour; put them into cold water, take off the shells, cut three of the whites and four yolks in small pieces, mix them with melted butter, and heat it well.

317.—Shrimp Sauce.

Pick some shrimps nicely from the shell, put them into melted butter, and add a tablespoonful of lemon pickle and vinegar; heat it.

318.—Mint Sauce.

Pick and wash some green mint; add, when minced, a tablespoonful of the young leaves to four of vinegar, and put it into a sauce-tureen, with a teaspoonful of brown sugar.

319.—Pudding Sauce.

Mix with half a pint of melted butter two wineglasses of sherry and a tablespoonful of pounded loaf sugar; make it quite hot, and serve in a sauce-tureen, with grated nutmeg on the top

320.—Parsley and Butter.

Pick and wash clean a large bunch of parsley, tie it up, and boil it for a few minutes in water; drain and chop it very finely, add some melted butter, and make it quite hot. It is better to be made thick with parsley.

321.—Melted Butter.

Dust a little flour over a quarter of a pound of butter, and put it into a saucepan, with about a wineglass of water; stir it one way constantly till it is melted, and let it just boil: a round wooden stick is the best thing to stir butter with in melting. If the butter is to be melted with cream, use the same proportion as of water, but no flour; stir it constantly, and heat it thoroughly, but do not let it boil.

322.—French Melted Butter.

Mix in a stewpan, with a quarter of a pound of fresh butter, a tablespoonful of flour, a little salt, half a gill of water, half a spoonful of white vinegar, and a litttle grated nutmeg. Put it on the fire, stir it, and let it thicken, but do not allow it to boil, lest it should taste of the flour.

323.—Stuffing for Hare or Kid.

Parboil the liver, and mince it; add an equal quantity of grated bread, double the quantity of fat bacon chopped, and a bit of butter the size of a walnut. Season with pepper, salt, nutmeg, chopped lemon thyme, and parsley; bind with an egg beaten.

324.—Stuffing peculiar for Fowls only.

Take four boiled potatoes; break them into pieces while hot, and add a chittack or two ounces of butter free of water, some pepper and salt, a little grated bread-crumb, and some eight or ten olives stoned, and cut or chopped small; the quantity of potatoes and bread-crumb may be increased or decreased according to the size of the fowl or number of fowls to be stuffed; moisten with a little stock or gravy before stuffing the fowls.

325.—Stuffing for Roast Pig, Roast Kid, Fillets of Veal, and Duck.

Break up, *but not mash*, six boiled potatoes with one chittack or two ounces of butter free of water; cut into fine slices two white Patna onions, take a little finely-chopped suet, finely-grated crumbs of a slice of stale bread, a teaspoonful of ground pepper, a teaspoonful of salt, all kinds of soup herbs, and a dessertspoonful of tomato or tapp sauce, add a little of the stock or gravy of the giblets, &c., and stuff the pig, kid, or bird. The quantity of potatoes may be increased or decreased according to the size of the roast to be stuffed.

N.B.—The liver may be cut up or minced, and added to the stuffing.

326.—Stuffing for Boiled Turkey, Goose, or Duck.

Mince a quarter of a pound of beef suet, and grate fine the crumb of a thick slice of stale bread; add a good quantity of soup herb, finely sliced and chopped Patna onions, lemon-peel, some grated nutmeg, a teaspoonful of white pepper, a teaspoonful of salt, half a dozen oysters, and an anchovy, or in the absence of anchovies a little minced ham or tongue; melt down one chittack or two ounces of butter; then throw in the above ingredients and warm up well; moisten with stock, and then stuff the bird.

327.—Stuffing for Roast Duck.

Slice into fine long strips or ribbons as much of the heart or inside of a young tender cabbage as will suffice for stuffing; wash and dry it through a colander, and shake it up in a napkin, without crushing or destroying the crispness of the leaves; take for the stuffing as much only as will suffice to stuff the number of ducks intended to be dressed; add for each duck a teaspoonful of finely-pounded pepper, and one of salt, with three cloves of garlick, and two chittacks or four ounces of butter free of water; stuff your birds and bake or roast as you please.

328.—Stuffing for Roast Turkey or Goose.

Break, blanch, and slice up very fine twenty-five Barcelona nuts and a dozen Jordan almonds, and set aside; fry, in two chittacks or four ounces of butter free of water, four tablespoonfuls of finely-sliced onions; add to it one dozen oysters, half a dozen boiled potatoes broken up small, but not mashed, a pork or beef sausage broken up small, the rind of a fresh lemon finely sliced and chopped, the crumb of a slice of stale bread grated fine, some garden herbs, grated nutmeg, plenty of finely-pounded pepper, and salt to taste; then add the sliced nuts, and as much stock as will cover the whole of the mixture, and allow it to simmer over a slow fire until it is reduced to the consistency of stuffing; next add the juice of a lemon and a little mushroom catsup and port wine, and stuff the bird, after fixing the stuffing with an egg.

329.—Jelly for Cooked Birds, Meats, or Made Dishes.

Boil down eight calves'-feet, with some pepper and salt, two onions, a head of celery, and two carrots, in three or four quarts of water, according to the quantity of jelly required; when perfectly boiled down strain it lightly without bruising the onions or carrots; let it cool, and remove all the fat; then, with a dozen cloves and the juice and rind of a lemon, boil it again, adding a tablespoonful of soy or any other dark-coloured, rich, and well-flavoured sauce; beat up to a light froth the whites of four eggs, and clear the soup or jelly; add a wineglass of brown sherry, and run or drip it through flannel. Pour what you require over the ready cooked or dressed meat into moulds, and let the rest cool in some large flat dish, and cut it up small for garnishing the meat or bird when served up.

INDIAN PICKLES, CHUTNEES, SAUCES, ETC.

330.—Love-apple or Tomato Sauce.

Ingredients:—Five hundred tomatoes; two pounds of green ginger, ground fine; a pound and a half of garlic, ground fine; one pound of chilies, ground fine; one pound of salt; three pounds of tamarinds; and three quarts of vinegar.

Steep the tamarinds for twelve hours in a quart of the vinegar; strain them through a sieve, rejecting the stones, and add the other two quarts of vinegar, all the ground condiments, and salt; break the tomatoes into the mixture, and boil the whole, stirring it all the time until it thickens; remove it from the fire, and when cold strain it carefully and bottle the liquid, which is the sauce.

331.—Tomato or Love-apple Chutnee.

Ingredients:—Two hundred large ripe love-apples, four ounces of raisins, seven ounces of salt, four ounces of sugar, eight ounces of chilies, finely sliced, four ounces of ground garlic, and seven ounces of ground mustard-seed.

Parboil the tomatoes in a quart of vinegar, add the other ingredients, and allow the whole to stand for ten to twelve hours; then boil it for twenty to thirty minutes over a slow fire; when cold, bottle it.

332.—Tapp Sauce.

Ingredients:—Three seers or six pounds of peeled and sliced mangoes, two pounds of ground raisins, a pound of ground garlic, half a pound of ground chilies, a pound and a half of ground ginger, a pound of sugar, two pounds of salt, a quart of lime-juice, and six quarts of vinegar.

Mix all the above well together, put it into stone jars, and expose it to the sun for twenty days or a month, after which drain away the liquid, which is the sauce; boil it for ten to fifteen minutes, and when cold bottle and cork it.

333.—Sweet Chutnee.

The refuse of the tapp sauce makes an excellent chutnee with the addition of some thick syrup, a few dried dates, a few more whole raisins, and some hot spices. Put the whole into a pan and let it simmer for a quarter of an hour, or until the syrup is absorbed and the chutnee reduced to a proper consistency; when cool, bottle, and cork it well down.

334.—*Another Way.*

Ingredients:—Two hundred green mangoes, peeled and sliced, four pounds of salt, three pounds of ground garlic, three pounds of ground ginger, one pound of chilies, finely sliced, four pounds of raisins, half a dozen bay-leaves, eight pounds of sugar, and four quarts of vinegar.

Make all the sugar into a syrup with two quarts of the vinegar, in which the sliced mangoes must be boiled; when half done, throw in the other ingredients, and mix up well; last of all, add the remaining two quarts of vinegar, and when the chutnee begins to thicken remove it from the fire; let it cool, and then bottle it.

335.—Sweet Mango Chutnee.

Ingredients:—A hundred green mangoes, peeled and sliced, two seers of tamarinds stoned, the syrup of six pounds of sugar boiled in three quarts of vinegar, one tablespoonful of finely-pounded cinnamon, two pounds of salt, two pounds of sliced ginger, two pounds of cleaned and picked raisins, three quarts of vinegar, and one dessertspoonful of grated nutmeg.

Peel the mangoes, cut them into fine slices, and steep them in salt for thirty-six hours; drain away the salt water, and boil them in the three quarts of vinegar; when cool, remove them into a preserving-pan, mix in all the condiments and other ingredients, and allow the whole to simmer for half an hour, pouring in the syrup gradually, and mixing all the time, until the vinegar and syrup have been absorbed, and the chutnee has acquired the desired consistency; bottle and cork when perfectly cold.

336.—Hot Sweet Mango Chutnee.

Ingredients:—A hundred green mangoes, the syrup of four pounds of sugar and three quarts of vinegar, four pounds of tamarinds, stoned and strained, three quarts of vinegar, eight or ten bay-leaves, one pound of ground chilies, two pounds of sliced ginger, one pound of cloves of garlic, one pound of raisins, and two pounds of salt.

Peel and cut the mangoes into fine slices, and steep them in salt for twenty-four to thirty-six hours; remove the mangoes from the salt water, and boil them in three quarts of vinegar; when quite cool, lay them in a preserving-pan, sprinkle over them the remaining salt, add all the condiments, tamarinds, raisins, &c., and allow the whole to simmer for half an hour, stirring all the time, with the syrup. It should not be bottled until quite cold.

337.—Tamarind Chutnee.

Ingredients:—Four pounds of ripe tamarinds without the stones, a quarter of a pound each of ground chilies, ginger, and garlic, two ounces of ground cinnamon, half a pound of picked currants, half a pound of raisins (the small Cabool are the best), two pounds of soft sugar, a quarter of a pound of salt, and a quart of vinegar.

Put the whole into a glazed earthen preserving-pan, pour over it a quart of vinegar or syrup, or as much as will entirely cover the mixture, and mix all well together; then allow it to simmer over a quick fire until the vinegar or syrup is absorbed and the chutnee thickened to the required consistency; it must be stirred during the whole time it is on the fire.

N.B.—The two pounds of sugar and the quart of vinegar may be made into syrup or used separately.

338.—Cussoondee.

Peel and slice fine a hundred green mangoes, steep them in salt for twelve hours, then put them under a heavy pressure for two hours, and drain away all the water; then mix with them half a pound each of ground chilies, ginger, and garlic, half a pound of bruised mustard-seed, two pounds of tamarinds without the stones, and some salt; when the whole is thoroughly mixed, pour over it as much warmed or cooked mustard oil as will entirely cover it, and cook it for ten to fifteen minutes over a brisk fire; when cold bottle it, taking care that it is kept several inches well under the oil, and that it is well corked, or it will spoil.

339.—Mango Amchoor.

Peel and quarter some green mangoes; sprinkle with salt, and expose them to the sun until they begin to dry up; then rub them with dry pounded turmeric, chilies, and dry ginger; sprinkle more salt, and expose them to the sun again, until they are quite dried up, when they may be bottled and kept for use.

340.—Pickled Cabbage.

Quarter a full-sized cabbage, keep it in salt for forty-eight hours, and then drain away all the water. Prepare a pickle or brine of salt and water in the proportion of eight ounces of salt to twenty-four ounces of water, and boil it with half an ounce each of peppercorns and bay-leaves; pack the cabbage loose in a wide-mouthed stone jar, and pour over it the cold pickle or brine, which should have been boiled the day before. Care must be taken to keep the mouth of the jar always airtight, or the cabbage will rot. When required for use, take out as much as will be required, steep it in fresh cold water for an hour or two, and then boil it the same as fresh cabbage.

341.—Red Cabbage Pickle.

Slice the cabbage, and sprinkle salt over each layer; after twenty-four hours remove it into a colander, and allow all the salt water to drain; then put the cabbage into a pan, pour in sufficient boiling vinegar to cover it, and add a few slices of red beetroot; when cold, put it into glass bottles and cork down.

342.—Red Cauliflower Pickle.

This is a very uncommon pickle, and looks particularly pretty in white bottles. Cut the cauliflower into pieces of equal sizes, sprinkle with salt and place it in the sun for a couple of days. Make a syrup of vinegar and sugar: to every quart of vinegar put a quarter of a pound of sugar, a few sticks of cinnamon, and as much sliced or bruised and pounded red beet as will give the vinegar a deep red colour. When all the salt water has drained away, put the cauliflower into a pan, and pour over it the boiling-hot vinegar or syrup through a fine sieve, in order to leave behind the sticks of cinnamon and fibres of the beetroot; when cold, put the pickle into nice white bottles and cork.

343.—Patna or Bombay Onion Pickle.

According to the size and number of bottles, take the small or button onions; remove the outer coat, wash and dry them thoroughly, throw them into a pan with some vinegar, and parboil them; set the vinegar aside, after filtering it, for shrimp, cucumber, and other salads, or for the preparation of mustard. Put the parboiled onions when cold into wide-mouthed bottles, laying them alternately with fresh red chilies, a few black peppercorns, some finely-sliced green ginger, and a little salt. Fill the bottles with vinegar, and cork them.

344.—Mangoes Pickled Whole.

Peel and divide some large-sized mangoes sufficiently to admit of the stones being easily extracted; rub them over with salt, and expose them to the sun for two or three days; then dry them with a napkin, and stuff each mango with a few cloves of garlic, finely-sliced chilies and ginger, some cullungee seeds, a clove or two, and a stick or two of cinnamon; tie them securely with strong sewing cotton, and put them into bottles, with vinegar sufficient to cover them; cork the bottles well, and expose them to the sun for fifteen to twenty days. The pickle will be ready for use in three or four months.

To prevent the pickle spoiling, it is not unusual to pour a tablespoonful or two of mustard oil over it when in the bottle.

345.—Sweet Mango Pickle.

Peel and quarter a hundred green mangoes, and steep them in salt for thirty-six hours; drain off the salt water, wipe the mangoes dry, and put them into a preserving-pan, with a seer or two pounds of sliced ginger, and half a seer of chilies finely sliced; pour in a syrup made of sugar and vinegar (half a seer of the former to two quarts of the latter), and allow the whole to simmer for ten to fifteen minutes; bottle when quite cold.

346.—Long Plum Pickle.

Take the long plums, or what the natives call *nar kollee bhyar;* remove the peel, and keep them in salt in the sun for a day or two; drain away the salt water, and put them into bottles, in layers alternately with fresh chilies, cloves of garlic, ginger finely sliced, and peppercorns; add a little more salt, and pour in as much vinegar as will cover the whole; cork and expose to the sun for fifteen to twenty days. This is one of the most delicious of Indian pickles; it will not be fit for use until the plums have pickled for six months.

347.—Sweet Long Plum Pickle

Is made in every respect according to the foregoing recipe, with the addition of a syrup in the proportion of a quarter of a pound of sugar to every quart of vinegar, and a few sticks of cinnamon.

348.—Round Plum Pickle.

Get the perfectly ripe fruit, which the natives call *cool;* put them into a damp cloth, and roll them about to free them of dust; sprinkle them well with salt, and stand them in the sun for three or four days; then drain away all the water, and bottle the plums alternately with cloves of garlic, green or fresh red chilies, sliced ginger, peppercorns, and ground mustard-seed; add a little salt, fill up the bottles with vinegar, and cork, and expose them to the sun for fifteen to twenty days.

349.—Round Plum Pickle with Mustard Oil

Is made like the above, the only difference being that some mustard oil is poured over the vinegar, and allowed to float about an eighth of an inch thick over the surface.

350.—Dry Fruit Pickle.

This is the pickle of all pickles. Take equal quantities of "dry dates," called the *shawarah, khobanee,* or Arabian apricots; *allobhokara,* a species of Arabian plum or damson; English prunes, rather of the dry sort; and Normandy dry pippins. Wash and clean them thoroughly, particularly the Arabian dry fruits, which are very dirty, and dry them well in the sun. Stew the dry dates for ten to fifteen minutes, cut them up into rings, and throw away the stones. Make a syrup of good French vinegar, in the proportion of a quarter of a pound of good clean sugar to a quart of French vinegar. After quartering the pippins, arrange them and the other fruit in a wide-mouthed bottle in alternate layers, with finely-sliced ginger, peppercorns, sticks of cinnamon, and small sprinklings of salt; then pour over the whole as much of the vinegar syrup as will entirely cover the fruit; cork the bottle well down, expose it in the sun for a few days, and it will be fit for use in a month.

351.—Green Mint Vinegar.

Put into a wide-mouthed bottle enough fresh, clean mint-leaves to fill it loosely, and fill it up with good vinegar. After it has been stopped close for two or three weeks, pour off the vinegar clear into another bottle, and keep it well corked for use. Serve with lamb or kid when fresh mint cannot be obtained.

352.—*Another Way.*

Fill a wide mouthed bottle with fresh, full-grown, green mint-leaves; pour in a quart of vinegar; after ten or fifteen days strain away the liquor, and re-fill the bottle with fresh leaves; pour back the liquor, and after it has steeped for ten or fifteen days longer, strain and bottle for use as required.

353.—Horseradish Vinegar

To three ounces of finely-scraped horseradish add a quart of vinegar and a drachm of cayenne, some black pepper and celery-seeds, and one ounce of bruised onions; after eight or ten days filter the vinegar, which will serve as an excellent relish for cold beef, salads, &c., and for the preparation of mustard.

354.—Chili Vinegar.

Pick, clean, and put into a glass-stoppered bottle one chittack or two ounces of birds'-eye chilies, and pour over them a pint and half of the best vinegar; after a month's time filter through blotting-paper a pint of the vinegar; add to what remains half a pint more of vinegar, and expose it to the sun for a few days, when the second portion will also be ready for use.

355.—Essence of Chilies.

Pick one chittack or two ounces of the best dried Patna chilies; expose them to a hot sun for an hour; then pound them to as fine a powder as possible; put the powder into a stoppered bottle with a teaspoonful of salt, pour over it as much vinegar only as will form a limp paste, and expose it to the sun for a few days; then pass it through muslin, adding to it as much more vinegar as will reduce it to the consistency of some thick sauce.

356.—To Preserve Lime-juice

Squeeze and strain a pint of lime-juice; put into a basin one pound of double-refined sugar finely pounded and sifted, add the lime-juice, and stir it with a silver spoon till the sugar is perfectly dissolved. Bottle it, and cork it tightly; seal the cork, or tie bladder over it, and keep it in a dry, cool place.

357.—To Purify Lime-juice.

To a quart of strained lime-juice add an ounce of well-burnt and finely-pounded animal charcoal; in twelve hours filter it through blotting-paper, and put it into small phials; cork these tightly, and keep them in a cool place; a thick crust will form beneath the corks, and the mucilage will fall to the bottom.

358.—Green Mint-juice.

If for immediate use, extract it with water, but if required to keep for a few days, take brandy for the purpose. Pick and clean half a dozen large stalks of good fresh mint, and pound the leaves in a mortar with a dessertspoonful of water, or with brandy, then put them into muslin and squeeze out all the liquor. Juice may be extracted a second time by a little more water or brandy being added, and the leaves rebruised and pressed through muslin.

359.—Green Ginger-juice

Is extracted in the same manner as mint-juice.

360.—Juice of Onions and Garlick

Is extracted by pounding the condiment in a mortar with a little water, and squeezing the juice through muslin.

361.—Mustard.

There are various ways of preparing mustard for the table, each with its admirers, yet in nine houses out of ten it is often so execrably done as to mar the best dinner, through the loss of its piquancy and pungency. Be the quantity ever so small, it should never be prepared in a cup, but in a soup or other deep plate. The dry mustard, with a little salt, should first be well rubbed down with the back of a spoon; the water, vinegar or other liquid should then be gradually added, and mixed gently until the required consistency has been obtained; it should then be mixed briskly, turning the spoon one way only, and in a few minutes the pungency of the mustard will tell on the eyes; put it immediately into the mustard-pot, *and cork it,* removing the cork only when the mustard is required for use. It is a mistake to suppose that the little silver or plated lid to a mustard-pot is intended, or is sufficient, to preserve the piquancy and pungency of the condiment. The practice which prevails in some houses of allowing the spoon to remain immersed in the mustard, which has probably been prepared with vinegar, the spoon perhaps being a plated one, is very objectionable.

It is scarcely necessary to give any further instructions, excepting that hot water should not be used. Some like mustard prepared simply with water; others prefer weak vinegar and water. It is also prepared with plain vinegar, with tarragon vinegar, with vinegar taken from pickles and capers, and with onion and garlick juice. The best mustard for roast beef is that prepared with horseradish; the most delicate flavoured is that made with tarragon vinegar, or vinegar taken from capers.

INDIAN PRESERVES, JAMS, JELLIES, AND MARMALADES.

HINTS ABOUT THE MAKING OF PRESERVES.

It is not generally known that boiling fruit a long time without sugar, in an open preserving-pan, and skimming it well, is a very economical way, as the whole of the scum rises from the fruit, and boiling without a cover allows the evaporation of all the watery particles. Preserves boiled in this way keep firm and well-flavoured. Jam made as above, with the addition of a quarter of a pound of good pure sugar to every pound of fruit, is excellent.

362.—To Detect Adulteration of Sugar.

The adulteration of brown sugar may be detected by dissolving a little in a glass of clear water: if sand or any similar substance be present, it will after a while fall to the bottom of the glass. If white sugar, adulterated with flour, chalk, or other similar substances, be dissolved in clear water, the latter will become opaque or discoloured, and a sediment will be formed at the bottom of the glass.

363.—White Syrup.

Put a quart of water over the fire in a well-tinned and clean copper stewpan; when on the boil, drop into it lump by lump one pound of the best loaf sugar; let it well boil up, and after all the sugar is thoroughly dissolved, pour it into a broad dish to cool. When cold it is fit for use.

364.—Brown Syrup.

Take a pound of brown sugar-candy called *misseree*, and prepare the syrup as directed above. After all the sugar is thoroughly dissolved, strain it through a sheet of stout blotting-paper spread on muslin, and allow the syrup to drip into a broad dish. Use it when quite cold.

365.—To Clarify Sugar.

To every three pounds of loaf sugar allow the beaten white of on egg and a pint and a half of water; break the sugar small, put it into a nicely cleaned brass pan, and pour the water over it; let it stand some time before it be put upon the fire; then add the beaten white of the egg, stir till the sugar be entirely dissolved, and when it boils up pour in a quarter of a pint of cold water, and let it boil up a second time; then remove it from the fire and let it settle for fifteen minutes; carefully take off all the scum, put it again on the fire, and boil till sufficiently thick, or, if required, till candy high: in order to ascertain this, drop a little from a spoon into a cup of cold water, and if it become quite hard, it is sufficiently done; or dip the handle of a wooden spoon into the sugar, plunge it into cold water, and draw off the sugar which adheres; if the sugar be hard and snaps, the fruit to be preserved must be instantly put in and boiled.

366.—Capillaire.

To a quart of water add three pounds of lump sugar, one pound of soft sugar, and the whites and yolks of two eggs well beaten up; boil it gently, and skim well; on the scum ceasing to rise, remove the pan from the fire, add two ounces of the best orange-flower water, and strain through flannel.

367.—Ceylon Moss, Seaweed, and Iceland Moss Preserves.

Steep the moss or weed for two or three days in fresh water, changing the water two or three times a day; wash it well once before boiling it; to every seer or two pounds of the weed add a wineglassful of the best vinegar; allow it to simmer over a gentle fire until it thickens, so as to congeal in a glass; then strain the moss or weed through a towel, pour the liquid into clarified sugar or syrup, and boil them together for half an hour; pour the jelly into large wide dishes, and when quite cold cut it into cakes. If desired, the jelly may be coloured or tinted with cochineal.

368.—Guava Jelly.

Select ripe guavas, and as they are peeled and quartered throw them into a large bowl of fresh clean water; then boil them in as much other clean water as will only cover the fruit, and when perfectly tender, so as to dissolve to the touch, strain through a fine sieve or towel without breaking or pressing the fruit, and allow it to drip through for twelve to eighteen or twenty-four hours if necessary. Put the juice on the fire again without a cover to the preserving-pan; boil and skim well; add gradually good clean sugar to your taste; when nearly done, add lime-juice in the proportion of ten large juicy limes to every hundred guavas; after it has boiled until no more scum rises, and the jelly is quite clear, pour it while the jelly is warm into glass or stone jars, and cork them down when quite cold. A hundred guavas will give two to two and a half jars of jelly, and will take from two to two and a half hours' cooking or boiling.

369.—Guava Cheese.

After all the water or juice has drained from the guavas boiled for jelly, pass the fruit or pulp through a sieve, rejecting the seeds; add lime-juice and sugar to taste, and boil over a slow fire to a consistency stiff enough for it to remain unmoved in a spoon; rub a little butter in a mould, fill it with the cheese while hot, and place it in a heat, or in an expiring oven, to dry; the colour may be improved with tne aid of cochineal.

370.—Mango Jelly.

Peel and stone a hundred green mangoes, and cut each into four, throwing them as they are ready into a solution of weak lime-water, strained of all sediment. When all have been peeled and stoned, remove them into a large vessel, pour in as much cold water as will entirely cover them, and boil them until they are quite dissolved; then carefully strain the liquid without pressing the fruit, and let it drip all night. Boil the juice again in an open preserving-pan, and cut away the scum as it rises; then add gradually good clean white sugar until it is sweetened to taste; continue to boil steadily until the scum has ceased to rise, and the jelly is quite clear and transparent; allow some of it to drop on a plate and cool; if it congeals, remove the pan and fill the bottles while the jelly is slightly warm, and cork down when quite cold.

371.—Mango Marmalade.

Pass through a sieve the pulp of the mangoes which had been boiled for jelly; add plenty of clean white sugar, without quite destroying the acidity of the fruit; boil it over a slow fire until it acquires the thickness of guava cheese, and bottle while it is yet warm.

N.B.—This marmalade is well adapted for rolly-polly puddings, tarts, mango fool, and the preparation of sauces for boiled goose, ducks, &c.

372.—Green Mango Preserve.

Select mangoes slightly under the middling size, taking care that they are not bruised or injured in any way. Steep them in clean water; grate the outer coat, or peel very finely, so as to remove thoroughly a fine coat of green from the surface; cut them sufficiently lengthways to extract the stones, and then throw them into lime-water. Remove them into a copper preserving-pan with clean water, and parboil them, skimming them well; throw them into a sieve, and allow all the water to drain away; have a large quantity of good syrup prepared, allowing two pounds of sugar to every twenty-five mangoes; throw the mangoes into the syrup, and allow them to simmer; cut away the scum until the sugar inclines to crystallize; then remove the pan from the fire, and put the preserve into wide-mouthed bottles; before corking them down, it will be necessary to examine the syrup every two or three days, and if it be found that it is becoming thin, it will have to be reboiled; just as the boiling is about to be finished, the mangoes ought to be put into it to warm up; this precaution must be taken every time the syrup has been reboiled, until there is no further appearance of fermentation; the bottles may then be securely corked down, and the preserve will keep good for years.

373.—*Another Way.*

Peel and stone good middling-sized green mangoes, and steep them in lime-water; parboil them in fresh water, and then in syrup until it thickens; put them into bottles, and examine them daily; if any signs of fermentation appear, reboil the syrup, and put in the fruit at the end of the boiling; the reboiling to be continued until the syrup has ceased to ferment.

The difference between this and the foregoing preserve is only in appearance: the former will be of a greenish tint, and the latter of a rich light brown.

N.B.—Care must be taken to have plenty of syrup at the starting, so that at the end of the two or three reboilings there may be enough left to cover the fruit.

374.—Pine-apple Preserve.

Take care that the pines are not green, nor yet quite ripe; remove the peel, cutting it deeply, and then all the seeds and eyes; cut each pine into six slices, lay them in a preserving-pan, and sprinkle over each layer a good quantity of sugar, a few sticks of cinnamon, and a few bay-leaves, covering the uppermost layer with a larger quantity of sugar; allow them to simmer over a tolerably brisk fire until the sugar has all melted; then reduce the fire, and continue to simmer until the pines have quite changed colour and become tender; remove them out of the syrup into a colander, and allow them to drain, but continue to boil the syrup with all that drops from the fruit until it has thickened; then return the fruit into the syrup and finish the boiling. Bottle when quite cool, but before corking them for good, ascertain the state of the syrup every two or three days; if it shows signs of fermentation, remove it from the fruit and reboil it; this operation must be continued until the syrup has ceased to ferment; the *fruit is not* to be reboiled, but only returned into the syrup when the boiling is about to be finished.

375.—*Another Way.*

Finish the preserve by boiling the sliced pines and sugar together until the fruit has become of quite a dark colour, and the syrup so thick that it is not likely to ferment. There is, however, the objection to this method that the fruit becomes more or less leathery, and is not mellow like that preserved according to the foregoing recipe.

376.—Peach Preserve.

Clean the peaches, slit them with a silver or plated knife, and remove the stones; have a very strong syrup ready, and while it is boiling hot throw in the peaches, and let them stand over a slow fire for six to eight hours; then remove them from the fire, and twelve hours after drain off the syrup and reboil it; return the fruit into the syrup, and if it shows any disposition to ferment, boil it again; when satisfied it will not ferment any more, add a little brandy, say a wineglassful to every fifty peaches, and boil the whole over a slow fire for two hours. Bottle when quite cold. The kernels from the stones may be put in if desired.

377.—*Another Way.*

Clean the peaches, and put them with the stones into a preserving-pan with sufficient water to cover them; allow them to simmer until quite tender, cutting away the scum, and then spread them on a dish to cool. Make a syrup, allowing three-quarters of a pound of sugar to every pound of fruit, and while it is boiling hot put in the peaches, and boil them gently until the syrup is quite thick. Two days after drain off the syrup and reboil it, returning the fruit into it while hot; if at the end of twenty-four or thirty-six hours it has become thin again, it must be reboiled; a little brandy should be added finally.

N.B.—If the peaches are boiled in two waters, the first may be thrown away, but the second, in which the peaches should be boiled a longer time, may be taken for making the syrup.

378.—Pulwal Preserve.

Take two seers or four pounds of large full-grown pulwals without any decay; peel, slit, remove the seeds, and throw them into cold water; wash them thoroughly, and parboil them in clean water; then put them in a colander, and set them aside to cool. Prepare a good strong syrup of half a seer of sugar and a quarter of a seer or half a pound of green ginger well bruised; throw the pulwals in, and allow them to simmer until the syrup thickens. They should be removed immediately the colour becomes quite brown, but the syrup must be kept boiling till it has acquired the proper consistency; return the pulwals into the syrup, and, if necessary, reboil it two or three days after, if it appears to have become thin, or inclined to ferment.

379.—*Another Way.*

Take two seers or four pounds of good large fresh pulwals; thoroughly grate the outer surface, half slit them, remove the seeds, and throw them into water; parboil them in clean water, remove them into a colander, and allow them to drain and dry; then stuff each pulwal with some bruised green ginger, tie or bind them with fine cotton, put them into a strong syrup made of half a seer of sugar, and allow them to simmer until they change colour; remove them, and continue to boil the syrup until it thickens; then return them into the syrup, and in two or three days reboil the syrup, if it has become thin, or appears inclined to ferment.

380.—Candied Pulwal.

The same process is observed as directed for pulwal preserve, the chief difference being that hot or boiling clarified sugar or syrup must be used, and the preserve exposed to the sun, spread out on fresh oiled paper, to dry.

381.—Tipparee (commonly called Gooseberry) Preserve.

Shell or remove the pods of the tipparees, and wipe away all dust; prick each with a bamboo or other wooden pin, and put them into a preserving-pan; strew some sugar over each layer of fruit, making the final layer of sugar thicker than the others, and simmer the whole until all the juice has been extracted, and the syrup has acquired such a consistency that it will congeal if dropped on a plate; then remove the preserve quickly from the fire, and bottle while warm.

382.—Tipparee Jelly.

Clean and prick the tipparees as in the foregoing recipe, and put them into a clean well-tinned stewpan, with as much water as will entirely cover them; boil them until all the juice has run out; strain the latter into a preserving-pan through fine muslin, without crushing the fruit, and allow it to simmer for a while, removing the scum; then add to it fine clean white sugar to taste, in small quantities at a time, skimming it well all the while; when nearly ready, put in the juice of two lemons strained through muslin; when the scum has ceased to rise, and the jelly is clear, remove the pan from the fire; bottle the jelly while it is warm, and cork when it is quite cold.

383.—Tipparee Cheese or Marmalade.

Take the fruit which had been boiled for jelly, and pass it through a fine sieve, leaving the skins behind; clean and prick a few more tipparees, and add them to the strained fruit; put the whole into a preserving-pan with sugar, and simmer until of a sufficient consistency to make into cheese; add some orange marmalade, in the proportion of a tablespoonful to every mould; with a feather damp the moulds with melted butter or sweet oil, and pour into them the cheese while quite hot; place them in cold water, and turn out the cheeses as soon as they are cool enough to retain their shape.

384.—To Preserve Tamarinds.

Rid the tamarinds of all the stones; put a layer of sugar in a wide-mouthed bottle, and over it a layer of stoned tamarinds, then another layer of sugar, and so on alternately until the bottle is full; the final layer must be a deep one of sugar. Tie the stopper down with oiled bladder. This will keep good for years, and prove serviceable when fresh tamarinds cannot be procured.

385.—Bael Preserve.

The fruit must be rather less than half ripe, to enable it to be cut into firm slices a quarter of an inch thick; carefully remove the seeds, together with the gum by which they are surrounded, and throw the slices into cold water; when all the bael is ready, remove it from the water, and simmer it in a strong syrup over a slow fire for half an hour, or until it has become of a rich light brown colour; bottle it when cool, taking care that the fruit is well covered with syrup.

386.—Bael Jam.

The fruit must be half ripe, all the seeds and gum carefully removed, and the pulp passed through a coarse sieve into a preserving-pan with the help of a little water; add sugar to taste, and simmer over a slow fire for half an hour, or until the fruit and sugar have acquired the consistency of jam; let it cool, and then bottle.

387.—Candied Bael.

The fruit should be selected as for the preserve, cut into slices, and the seeds and gum removed; after steeping it in cold water, drain it, and put it in a preserving-pan, with sufficient boiling clarified sugar or syrup to cover it; simmer it over a slow fire for half an hour, or until it becomes quite tender; then remove the pan from the fire, lay the fruit on some fresh oiled paper spread on tin trays, and expose it to the sun; it will crystallize in a few hours, and the oil will prevent it adhering to the paper.

388.—Orange Jelly.

Melt an ounce and a half of isinglass and three-quarters of a pound of fine white sugar in a pint of water; add some orange and lemon peel, and boil until it is a good syrup; while warm, add the juice of ten oranges and two lemons, strain the whole through flannel, and put it into moulds. The juice of the fruit should not be boiled.

389.—Damson Cheese.

Take damsons that have been bottled for tarts, pass them through a sieve, and reject the skins and stones; to every pound of the strained pulp add half a pound of loaf sugar broken small; boil the whole until it has thickened; then pour it into buttered moulds and put it in an oven or warm place to dry; when quite firm, remove it from the moulds and serve up.

390.—Apricot Cheese.

Take the Cabool apricots, or those preserved for tarts; if the former, wash them thoroughly in several waters, parboil and reduce them to a pulp, and pass them through a sieve, rejecting all the skin, &c.; add sugar as directed in the foregoing recipe, and a handful or two of the apricot stones blanched, and boil the whole until it has thickened sufficiently; then pour it into buttered moulds, put it into an expiring oven or some warm place to dry, and when quite firm turn it out of the moulds.

N.B.—Other bottled fruits sent out to this country for tarts, *not preserved in sugar*, are admirably adapted for converting into marmalades, or for making into "fools."

391.—Orange Marmalade.

Take twenty-four oranges and six lemons, and of the best sugar a quantity equal to the weight of the fruit; grate the rinds of the oranges and lemons; then mark or cut into quarters and strip off the rinds without hurting the pulps; stew the rinds until they become perfectly tender, changing the water two or three times; then drain them, scrape out a little of the inside, and cut them into very fine slices or chips; next separate the pips, skin, and fibrous parts from the pulps, over which pour some water and strain it off; with this and a little more water prepare a syrup in a preserving-pan, add to it the whites of two eggs well beaten up, skim it well, and the moment it begins to boil take it off the fire; continue to remove the scum, add a little more water, boil, and strain until the syrup is perfectly clear; then throw in the chips and boil until they are quite transparent; next put in all the pulp and juice, and boil until it thickens. To ascertain if it has been sufficiently cooked, drop a little on a plate and see if it congeals.

392.—*Another Way.*

Stew good fresh ripe oranges till perfectly tender, changing the water several times; drain them, and cut and remove the rinds without breaking them or wounding the pulps; weigh the pulps, having previously removed all the pips, skin, and seeds, and to every six pounds of fruit add seven of sugar; pour boiling water over the pips, seeds, &c., strain them, and take the liquor for the preparation of syrup; skim it well while boiling; when clear, add to it the rind, having first scraped and thrown away some of the inside and then cut it up into thin slices or chips. After a while add the pulp and juice, and boil it up again until it acquires the consistency of jelly. This is a new method, and approved by some as being excellent and economical.

393.—Indian Way of Making Calf's-Foot Jelly.

Take twelve large or full-sized calves'-feet, one pound or half a seer of sugar, eight limes, two oranges, half a dozen blades of lemon-grass, a tablespoonful of mixed spices (say cinnamon, cardamoms, mace, nutmeg, and cloves), six eggs, a handful of isinglass, and a claretglassful of sherry. Having thoroughly washed the feet, break them up and boil them; allow all the meat to dissolve over a slow fire, skim away every particle of fat, and strain the liquid through a coarse napkin; add the sugar, all the hot spices, and the rinds of two lemons and one orange; simmer the whole for some time, squeeze in the juice of the eight limes and the two oranges, together with the isinglass and lemon-grass, and when it begins to thicken strain it; then reboil until it is reduced to the required quantity, skimming all the fat. Beat the whites of the six eggs to a good light froth; add this to the jelly, and pour it from one pan into another several times, until it clears; then add the sherry and strain it through flannel, returning it quickly two or three times until it runs perfectly bright and clear; fill into glasses or moulds before it quickly

HOME-MADE LIQUEURS.

394.—Cream of Citron.

Put sixty drops of the oil of citron into a quart of spirits of wine of the strength of sixty-two degrees overproof; shake it well, mix with it a quart of syrup and two ounces of yellow colouring matter, and filter the whole through filtering-paper. If not sufficiently bright, filter it a second time through some fresh paper, and bottle it.

395.—Cream of Cloves.

To a quart of spirits of wine of the strength given in the foregoing recipe add forty drops of oil of cloves; shake it well, and mix with it a quart of syrup, and as much yellow colouring matter as will give it a good colour; filter through filtering-paper and bottle immediately. It is a delightful liqueur, and is excellent for relaxed throats.

396.—Cream of Noyau.

To a quart of spirits of wine sixty-two degrees overproof add twenty drops of good essential oil of bitter almonds and six drops of oil of orange; shake it well, and add a quart of syrup; filter it through paper until it is quite clear.

397.—Pink Noyau.

To a quart of spirits of wine sixty-two degrees overproof add fifteen drops of essential oil of bitter almonds, three drops of oil of roses, four drops of oil of aniseed, and one drop of tincture of vanilla; shake it well, and mix with it a quart of syrup and a sufficient quantity of pink colouring matter to make it of a delicate pink colour: bottle it after filtering.

398.—Cream of Aniseed.

Put twenty drops of essential oil of aniseed in a quart of spirits of wine; after shaking it well, mix with it a quart of syrup; filter and put it in bottles.

399.—Cream of Cinnamon.

To a quart of spirits of wine add two drops of oil of cinnamon and two of oil of roses; shake it well until the oil has thoroughly dissolved, and add a quart of syrup and a sufficient quantity of red tincture to produce a bright full colour; it may then be filtered and bottled. This is an agreeable liqueur, and beneficial to dyspeptic persons.

400.—Rose Cream.

Into a quart of spirits of wine put twelve drops of the oil of roses and three of oil of nutmeg; shake the mixture well until the oils are dissolved, and add a quart of syrup, and a sufficient quantity of pink tincture to produce a fine rose-colour: filter and bottle.

401.—Cream of Mint.

Drop into a quart of spirits of wine twenty-five drops of oil of mint and three of oil of citron; shake it well, and add a quart of syrup and as much green colouring tincture as may be necessary: filter and bottle.

402.—Cream of Vanilla.

Put twelve drops of tincture of vanilla into a quart of spirits of wine; shake it well, and add a quart of syrup; when well mixed, let it stand for a quarter of an hour; then filter it two or three times through filtering paper, but do not filter again if it comes out bright and clear the first time. This is a most delicious cordial.

403.—Golden Wasser or Dantzic Brandy.

To a quart of spirits of wine add twelve drops of oil of aniseed, six of oil of cinnamon, three of oil of roses, and eight of oil of citron; shake it well until the oils dissolve; then add a quart of syrup, and filter through filtering-paper: before bottling the liqueur, stir into it a few squares of leaf-gold cut into very little bits.

404.—Curacao.

Boil a quart of water in a very clean pan, and add to it, bit by bit, a pound of dark brown sugar-candy; when the latter is dissolved, increase the fire and let the syrup boil up; then pour it into a deep dish to cool; dissolve a hundred and twenty drops of oil of bitter orange in a quart of spirits of wine sixty-two degrees overproof, and mix with the syrup when quite cold; then filter and bottle the liqueur.

This is a most difficult liqueur to filter of a clear bright colour; indeed, all liqueurs in which essential oils extracted from peals of the lemon tribe are used become so opaque on being mixed with syrup that the filtering is rendered a most tedious undertaking.

The proportions given in the above recipes are for the production of really good strong liqueurs, which will keep good for years, and improve by age. Liqueurs for immediate consumption need not be made quite so strong, two parts of syrup and one of spirits of wine will usually be sufficient; but consumers will be the best judges of their own tastes. A caution is very necessary against the free use of the essential oils: they are all harmless in moderation, but poison if used in excess, and some more powerful than others.

405.—Punch a la Romain.

Squeeze the juice out of eight juicy limes and four lemons or oranges strain it through muslin, and well mix with it two pounds of the best loaf sugar; beat to a light froth the whites of ten fresh eggs, and add gradually to the sugared juice; pour the whole into a pewter vessel, and place it in a tub containing two seers of *cutcha*, or raw ice, stirring it frequently to make it congeal. Ice two quarts of champagne, and when required add it to the contents of the pewter vessel; mix all well together, and serve in green or amber-coloured hock glasses. The addition of a little rum is considered an improvement.

406.—Mint Beer.

Put some bruised fresh-gathered mint-leaves into a large tankard, and pour over them a bottle of beer well iced, and a soda-water bottle of sparkling lemonade, also well iced; or use bottled mint-juice if the beer and lemonade have not been iced, and stir in a quarter of a pound of crushed ice.

407.—*Another Way.*

To the juice or bruised leaves add sufficient sugar to sweeten, and pour into the tankard two tumblers of water and two quarts of beer; stir and serve up with crushed ice, or cool the beer and water before the preparation.

408.—Ginger Beer.

Use bruised green ginger instead of mint, and ginger beer instead of lemonade.

409.—"The Commander-in-Chief."

Empty into a punchbowl a quart of claret and a bottle of soda-water; add a wineglassful of curaçao, and sweeten to taste with sugar; then throw in a handful of picked and bruised mint-leaves, with a seer of crushed ice; add a quart of champagne, stir briskly, and serve up.

410.—Regent Punch.

Mix a quart of sparkling champagne, a claretglassful of brandy, a wineglassful of old Jamaica rum, and a pint of very strong *pure green* tea; sweeten to taste with capillaire or any other syrup.

411.—Milk Punch.

Six quarts of rum and one of brandy, one quart of lime-juice, two seers of soft sugar, three quarts of cold water, two seers of pure milk, the rinds of forty limes, and three nutmegs will make twelve quarts of punch, as follows:—

Steep for two days in a bottle of the rum the peels of the forty limes; boil in the three quarts of water the two seers of soft sugar, and grate in the nutmeg; pour all the rum and syrup into a large vessel, and add gradually the quart of lime-juice and two seers of milk, boiling hot, stirring the whole time; let it stand for an hour or two, then strain through flannel several times until it drips clear, and bottle.

412.—*Another Way.*

Sixteen bottles of rum, three bottles of brandy, four bottles of lime-juice, eight bottles of milk, twelve bottles of water, eight seers of sugar, eight nutmegs, and the rinds of eighty limes, will make thirty-six quarts of milk punch, but of a milder quality than the foregoing.

The addition of a bottle of curaçao to milk punch is a great improvement: it may be added after the milk and lime-juice.

413.—Ginger Pop.

Boil an ounce of well-bruised green ginger cleaned of all rind, an ounce of cream of tartar, a pound of white sugar, some toddy, and some of the rind and all the juice of a large lime, in four quarts of water, for twenty minutes; when nearly cold, add a claretglassful of good fresh toddy; let it stand for six hours, and then put into soda-water bottles. It will fill eight or nine bottles.

414.—Imperial Pop.

Take three ounces of cream of tartar, an ounce of bruised ginger, a pound and a half of white sugar, and an ounce of lemon-juice, and pour a gallon and a half of boiling water on them, with two tablespoonfuls of yeast. Mix, bottle, and tie down the corks as usual.

415.—Negus.

To two quarts of claret or one of port add a wineglassful of brandy, two limes cut into thin slices, a slight grating of nutmeg, a few cloves, cardamoms, and sticks of cinnamon, two teacupfuls of boiling water, and two tablespoonfuls of sugar.

416.—Flash.

Mix half a pint of lemon ice with a wineglassful of Jamaica rum; pour over it, stirring briskly, a bottle of iced ginger beer; drink it while it is effervescing.

417.—Sherry Cobbler.

Pour into a tumbler two wineglassfuls of sherry, half a wineglassful of rum, and half a wineglassful of maraschino; add half an orange sliced fine, and fill the tumbler with crushed ice; take the preparation through a reed, quill, or common straw.

418.—Apricot Effervescing Drink.

Filter until clear a pint of the juice of bruised apricots, and make into a syrup with half a pound of sugar; then add an ounce of tartaric acid;

bottle, and cork well. To a tumbler three parts full of water add two tablespoonfuls of the syrup and a scruple of carbonate of soda; stir well, and drink while effervescing.

419.—Mint Julep.

Put about a dozen of the young sprigs of mint into a tumbler; add a tablespoonful of white sugar, half a wineglassful of peach, and the same of common brandy; then fill up the tumbler with pounded ice.

420.—Orangeade.

Squeeze out the juice of an orange; pour boiling water on a little of the peel, and cover it close; boil water and sugar to a thin syrup, and skim it; when cold, mix all together with as much water as will make a rich drink; strain through a jelly-bag, and ice.

421.—Orgeat.

Blanch and pound three-quarters of a pound of sweet and thirty bitter almonds with a tablespoonful of water; stir in by degrees two pints of water and three pints of milk, and strain the whole through a cloth; dissolve half a pound of loaf sugar in a pint of water; boil, skim well, and mix with the almond-water, adding two tablespoonfuls of orange-flower water and a teacupful of good brandy.

422.—Poor Man's Champagne.

Put a pint of Scotch ale into a jug, and add a bottle of good ginger beer.

423.—Royal Lemonade.

Pare two oranges and six lemons as thin as possible, and steep them four hours in a quart of hot water; boil a pound and a quarter of loaf sugar in three pints of water; skim it and add to the two liquors the juice of six oranges and a dozen lemons; stir well; strain through a jelly-bag, and ice.

424.—Summer Beverage.

Pour, while hot, two quarts of barley-water, made as in recipe 426, on the juice and rind of a lemon very thinly cut; to which add honey, capillaire, or sugar, according to taste; let it stand one hour and strain.

425.—Lemon Barley-water.

Two tablespoonfuls of pearl barley, a quarter of a pound of lump sugar, rather more than two quarts of boiling water, and the peel of a fresh lemon make a pleasant drink for summer. It should stand all night, and be strained the next morning.

MEDICINAL AND OTHER RECIPES.

426.—Barley-water for the Sick Chamber.

Mix smoothly a teaspoonful of Robinson's patent barley and a tablespoonful of cold spring water into a smooth paste, and gradually add a quart of boiling water; boil it gently for ten minutes, stirring constantly, and strain when cold.

427.—To Cure the Sting of a Wasp.

Oil of tartar or solution of potash applied to the part affected will give instant relief.

428.—To Cure Deafness from Deficient Secretion of Wax.

Mix half a drachm of oil of turpentine and two drachms of olive oil Put two drops into the ear at bedtime.

429.—Cure for Cramp in the Legs.

Stretch out the heels and draw up the toes as far as possible. This will often stop a fit of the cramp after it has commenced.

430.—Emetic Draught.

Mix one grain of emetic tartar, fifteen grains of powder of ipecacuanha, and an ounce and a half of water. This is commonly employed for unloading the stomach on the accession of fevers, and in ordinary cases.

431.—*Another Recipe.*

Mix ten grains of blue vitriol (sulphate of copper) and two ounces of distilled water.

432.—*Another Recipe.*

For a draught to be taken directly, mix a scruple of subcarbonate of ammonia, half a drachm of ipecacuanha in powder, three ounces of peppermint water, and two drachms of tincture of cayenne pepper. In case of poisoning, this is said to be more certain and effectual in arousing the action of the stomach than either of the preceding draughts.

433.—Cure for Tic-doloreux or Neuralgia.

Mix half a pint of rose-water and two teaspoonfuls of white vinegar. Apply it to the part affected three or four times a day: fresh linen should be used at each application. This will, in two or three days, gradually take the pain away.

At least three hundred "infallible cures" for tic-doloreux have been discovered, but the disease arises from such various causes that no remedy can be relied upon. Carbonate of iron cures one; quinine, another; upon a third neither has any effect. The remedy above suggested, although safe and simple, takes time to afford relief. Ten to twenty drops of Collis Browne's chlorodyne have been found from repeated experience to afford nearly instantaneous relief, and in some cases subject to periodical return to have effected almost perfect cures.

434.—To Cure Hiccough or Hiccup.

This spasm is caused by flatulency, indigestion, and acidity. It may generally be relieved by a sudden fright or surprise, or the application of cold, also by swallowing two or three mouthfuls of cold water or a teaspoonful of vinegar, or by eating a small piece of ice, taking a pinch of snuff, or anything that excites coughing.

435.—Cure for Colds.

Total abstinence from liquid food of any kind for a day or two (known as the dry system) has been known to cure coughs and colds where it has been persevered in.

436.—Mixture for Recent Coughs.

Mix five ounces of honey, a quarter of a pound of treacle, and seven ounces of best vinegar, and simmer in a common pipkin for fifteen minutes; remove it from the fire, and when the mixture has become lukewarm, add two drachms of ipecacuanha wine. The dose is a tablespoonful every four hours for adults. This is one of the best mixtures known for recent cough, and, on account of its pleasant taste, is particularly eligible for children and infants.

437.—Emulsion for Recent Coughs.

Mix an ounce of oil of sweet almonds, the yolk of one egg, five ounces of orange-flower water, half an ounce of mucilage of gum Arabic, a drachm and a half of ipecacuanha wine, and half an ounce of syrup of marshmallows. The dose is a tablespoonful when the cough is troublesome. Half this quantity may be given to young children.

438.—Emulsion for Old Coughs.

Rub well two drachms of gum ammoniac, gradually adding half a pint of water; when they are thoroughly mixed, strain them through linen.

This is a useful expectorant in old coughs and asthmas, when no inflammatory symptoms are present. The dose is from one to two tablespoonfuls, united with an equal quantity of almond emulsion.

439.—Cure for Hooping-cough.

Dissolve a scruple of salts of tartar in a quarter of a pint of water; add ten grains of cochineal, and sweeten with sugar. Give to an infant the fourth part of a tablespoonful four times a day; two years old, half a spoonful; from four years, a tablespoonful.

440.—Roche's Embrocation for Hooping-cough.

Mix eight ounces of olive oil, four ounces of oil of amber, and a sufficient quantity of oil of cloves to scent it strongly. This is the same as the famous embrocation of Roche. When rubbed on the chest, it stimulates the skin gently, and is sometimes serviceable in hooping-cough and the other coughs of children. In hooping-cough it should not be used for the first ten days of the disease.

441.—Valuable Lotion for Hooping-cough, &c.

Dissolve one drachm of emetic tartar in two ounces of common water, and add half an ounce of tincture of Spanish fly. This is a valuable lotion in the advanced stages of hooping-cough, and is of much service in all other coughs, both of adults and children. It is often very useful in removing the distressing cough and oppression of the chest left after the hoop has quitted the patient. After it has been rubbed into the chest night and morning for about a week, it will create a redness, and bring out some small pustules; it should then be applied only once a day, and if the part becomes very sore, it may be laid aside altogether, and the pustules anointed twice a day with simple white ointment. In very severe cases, however, it will be necessary to continue the use of this lotion until a large number of pustules appear; and if they are kept discharging freely by an occasional use of it, the relief will be more striking and permanent.

442.—Warm Plaster.

Melt together with a moderate heat one part of blistering plaster and fourteen of Burgundy pitch, and mix them so as to form a plaster. This will be stimulant, and create a slight irritation on the part to which it is applied. It is used with advantage in common cough, hooping-cough, sciatica, and local pain.

443.—Gargle for Irritation and Inflammation in the Throat.

Mix two drachms of purified nitre, seven ounces of barley-water, and seven drachms of acetate of honey. Use frequently.

444.—*Another Recipe.*

Mix half a drachm of muriatic acid and seven ounces of decoction of black-currant leaves or barley-water. This and the preceding gargle should be used when the object is to reduce the inflammation in the throat without its proceeding to suppuration. They are likewise useful in relaxed sore throat. This gargle possesses cleansing qualities, and should be used when the fauces are clogged with viscid mucus. It may be made still more detergent, if necessary, by increasing a little the quantity of acid.

445.—A Good Gargle for Sore Throats.

Mix two drachms of tincture of myrrh, four ounces of water, and half an ounce of vinegar.

446.—Excellent Domestic Gargle.

Mix together, in a half-pint tumbler, three teaspoonfuls of vinegar, two of tincture of myrrh, two of honey, and about one-fourth of a tumbler of port wine; then fill up the tumbler with lukewarm water, and the gargle will be fit for use. This is both pleasant and efficacious in all cases of sore throat. If a decoction of black-currant leaves be used instead of lukewarm water, it will be much improved.

447.—Remedy for Sprains.

Mix together one ounce each of camphorated spirit, common vinegar, and spirits of turpentine.

448.—*Another Recipe.*

Put the white of an egg into a saucer, and stir it with a piece of alum, about the size of a walnut, until it becomes a thick jelly; apply a portion of it on a piece of lint or tow large enough to cover the sprain, changing it for a fresh one as often as it gets warm or dry, and keep the limb in a horizontal position.

449.—Embrocation for Sprains and Bruises.

Mix together an ounce and a half of compound liniment of camphor and half an ounce of tincture of opium. This is a very useful application to sprains and bruises, after all inflammation has disappeared, and for rheumatic pains. Warmed and rubbed over the surface of the abdomen, it is of much service in allaying the pain of colic unattended by inflammation.

450.—*Another Recipe.*

Mix an ounce of solution of acetate of ammonia and an ounce of soap liniment. This is useful when the bruises or sprains are accompanied with inflammation.

451.—Lime Liniment for Burns, Scalds, &c.

Mix together equal parts of linseed or common olive oil and lime-water. Well shake the liniment every time it is used.

452.—Spermaceti Ointment for Dressing Blisters.

Melt an ounce of white wax and a quarter of an ounce of spermaceti in two ounces of olive oil, and stir the mixture till it becomes cold.

453.—To Prevent Galling in Persons confined to their Beds.

Beat the white of an egg to a strong froth, and gradually drop in two teaspoonfuls of spirits of wine; put the mixture into a bottle, and apply occasionally with a feather.

454.—Anodyne Fomentation.

Boil three ounces of white poppy-heads, half an ounce of elder-flowers, and three pints of water till one pint is evaporated; then strain out the liquor. This fomentation is used to relax spasm and relieve acute pain. Sometimes it may be advisable to add three teaspoonfuls of tincture of opium to it.

455.—Common Fomentation.

Boil an ounce of dried mallows, half an ounce of dried camomile-flowers, and a pint of water for a quarter of an hour, and strain. This is a very good fomentation for all common occasions.

456.—Nitric Acid Lotion.

Mix together two drachms of diluted nitric acid and a pint of water. This lotion is stimulating and detergent, and is very serviceable when applied to foul fœtid ulcers attended with a thin ichorous discharge. It is also useful in caries of the bone, and when there is an impending mortification. It is a favourite lotion in unhealthy ulcerations, which require the application of a mild stimulant.

457.—Cure for Bowel Complaint.

Mix half a drachm of rhubarb powder, a drachm of calcined magnesia, an ounce of paregoric elixir, and half a pint of peppermint water. Shake up, and take two tablespoonfuls every three hours till relieved.

458.—*Another Recipe.*

The following is a better prescription for the same purpose:—Mix eight ounces of chalk mixture, a drachm of aromatic confection, three drachms of compound tincture of camphor, and three or four drops of oil of caraways. Take two tablespoonfuls every three hours, or oftener if the pain and purging be urgent; a teaspoonful is a dose for young children, and one tablespoonful for those of ten or twelve years of age.

459.—Compound Infusion of Senna.

Macerate for an hour in a pint of boiling water, in a lightly covered vessel, an ounce and a half of senna-leaves and a drachm of sliced ginger-root, and strain the liquor. This is a useful purging infusion, in common use among medical men. It is usually given in conjunction with a little Epsom or Glauber's salts, and forms a purging mixture of great service in all acute diseases.

460.—Warm Purgative Tincture.

Put three ounces of senna-leaves, three drachms of bruised caraway-seeds, a drachm of cardamom-seeds, and four ounces of stoned raisins into two pints of best brandy; macerate for fourteen days in a gentle heat, and filter. This is quite equal to the celebrated Daffy's elixir, and is similar to the tincture of senna sold at the shops. It is stomachic and purgative, and is beneficially employed in flatulency, pains in the bowels, gouty habits, and as an opening medicine for those whose bowels have been weakened by intemperance. The dose is one, two, or three table-spoonfuls, in any agreeable vehicle.

461.—Tonic Aperient Mixture.

Mix three ounces and a half each of decoction of bark and infusion of senna, three drachms of sulphate of potash, and half an ounce of compound tincture of bark. Take three tablespoonfuls once or twice a day, so as to keep the bowels regular; or it may be used only occasionally, when an aperient is required.

462.—Mild Aperient Pills.

Beat into a mass and divide into twelve pills half a drachm of compound extract of colocynth, a scruple of compound rhubarb pill, ten drains of Castille soap, and five drops of oil of juniper. These are excellent aperient pills for occasional use in costiveness, bilious affections, and on all ordinary occasions, and are suited to the relief of these complaints in children as well as in adults. One pill taken at bedtime is generally sufficient, but some persons may require two.

463.—Digestive Aperient Pills.

Well rub thirty-six or forty grains of socotrine aloes with eighteen grains of gum mastic, and add twenty-four grains each of compound extract of gentian and compound galbanum pill, and a sufficient quantity of oil of aniseed to make twenty pills. Take two or three, an hour before dinner, or at night. They are stomachic and aperient, containing an antispasmodic, and producing usually a full feculent evacuation. They are very suitable to persons who have no vital energy to spare, and require a medicine which will operate mildly, surely, and safely.

464.—Worm Powder.

Rub well together two or three grains of calomel and ten grains of compound powder of scammony. This is an efficacious powder for the expulsion of worms from children and adults, and may be given twice a week, or oftener, till the object be accomplished.

465.—Infallible Cure for Tapeworm.

Take of the plant *Gisekia pharmaceoides*, in its green, fresh state, leaves, stalks, seeds, and seed-capsules (if the plant be in seed or forming its seed-vessels) indiscriminately one pound, and grind it down with sufficient water to render it liquid. It should be administered to the patient after twelve hours of fasting, and repeated on the fourth and eighth days. As a precautionary measure, to destroy any latent germs, repeat the dose in eight days more. The *Gisekia* is free of every poisonous quality: it simply possesses an acrid volatile principle, fatal alone to the tapeworm, and is in no way distressing to the stomach or digestive organs. The plant flourishes most luxuriantly in the jungles at Ferozepore, cis-Sutlej territories, Cawnpore, Seharunpore, Egypt, Coromandel, the banks of the Irrawaddie, in Burmah, and throughout Oude. As a specific it was first brought to European notice by a fakeer at Ferozepore, about the year 1856.

N.B.—The dried plant is useless.

466.—Cure for Ringworm.

The parts should be washed twice a day with soft soap and warm water; when dry, rub them with a piece of linen rag dipped in ammonia from gas tar; the patient should take a little sulphur and treacle, or some other gentle aperient, every morning; brushes and combs should be washed every day, and the ammonia kept tightly corked.

467.—Quinine Draught.

For dyspepsia and hepatic derangement mix two grains of sulphate of quinine, two drops of diluted sulphuric acid, one drachm of spirit of nutmegs, and ten drachms of distilled water, and take daily at midday.

468.—Seidlitz Powders.

Two drachms of tartarized soda and two scruples of bicarbonate of soda for the blue paper; thirty grains of tartaric acid for the white paper.

469.—Ginger-beer Powders.

Half a drachm of bicarbonate of soda, with a grain or two of powdered ginger and a quarter of an ounce of sugar, for the blue paper; twenty-five grains of tartaric acid for the white paper.

470.—Lemonade Powders.

Omit the ginger powder from the above, and to the water add a little essence of lemon or lemon-juice.

PERFUMERY, COSMETICS, AND DENTIFRICE.

471.—Indian Mode of Preparing Perfumed Oils.

The natives never make use of distillation. The plan adopted is to place on a large tray a layer of the flowers, about four inches thick and two feet square; on this they put some of the til or sesamum seed, wetted or damped, about two inches thick; on this, again, is placed another layer of flowers, four inches thick; the whole is then covered with a sheet, held down by weights at the sides, and allowed to remain for eighteen hours. The flowers are then removed and replaced by layers of fresh flowers, and the operation repeated three times, each layer of fresh flowers being allowed to remain eighteen hours. After the last process, the seeds are taken in their swollen state and placed in a clean mill; the oil then expressed possesses most fully the scent of the flowers. It is kept in prepared skins, called *dubbers*, and sold at so much per seer. The jasmine, bela, and chumbræl are the flowers from which the natives chiefly produce the oil.

472.—Remedy for Scurf in the Head.

Drop a lump of fresh quicklime the size of a walnut into a pint of water, and let it stand all night; pour the water off clear from sediment, add a quarter of a pint of the best vinegar, and wash the head with the mixture. It is perfectly harmless; only the roots of the hair need be wetted.

473.—Imitative Bears' Grease.

Melt together until combined eight ounces of hogs' lard and one-eighth of an ounce each of flowers of benzoin and palm oil; stir until cold, and scent at pleasure. This will keep a long time.

474.—Hair Grease.

Dissolve a quarter of a pound of lard in a basin of boiling water; when cold, strain off the water and squeeze the lard dry in a cloth; after which melt it in a pipkin, and mix well with it three tablespoonfuls of salad oil and enough palm oil to give it a colour. When cold, or nearly so, scent it and put it into pots. A little white wax may be added to make it thicker or stiffer.

475.—Pomatum.

Take a pound of white mutton suet, well boiled in a quart of hot water, and washed to free it from salt, &c.; when dried, melt it with half a pound of fresh lard and a quarter of a pound of bees' wax; pour it into an earthen vessel, and stir till it is cold; then beat into it fifteen drops of oil of cloves, or any essential oil whose scent is preferred. If too hard, use less wax.

476.—*Another Recipe.*

Take four ounces of lard, an ounce of castor oil, a quarter of an ounce of spermaceti, an ounce and a half of salad oil, a quarter of an ounce of white wax, a drachm and a half of tincture of lytæ, and twenty drops of oil of roses, verbena, bergamot, or cloves. Melt the wax, spermaceti, and lard with the oils in a glazed earthen pipkin, and when nearly cold add the scent.

477.—Pomade for Hair that is Falling off.

Take eight ounces of beef marrow, twenty-two drops of tincture of cantharides, sixty grains of sugar of lead, an ounce of spirits of wine, and twenty drops of oil of bergamot. Boil the marrow in the bone, and mix the prescribed quantity, free of bone and fibre, with the other ingredients, excepting the scent, which is to be added last of all; if any other scent be preferred, the bergamot may be omitted.

478.—Pomade Divine.

This is a capital pomade for rubbing into bruises, or to give relief in any similar hurt:—Take a pound and a half of beef marrow, which will be the produce of six or eight bones; clear it thoroughly from bone and fibre, and put it in an earthen vessel of spring water; change the water every night and morning for eight or ten days; then steep the marrow in a pint of rose-water for twenty-four hours, and drain it dry through a linen cloth. Take an ounce of flowers of benzoin, cyprus-root, odoriferous thorn, and Florentine iris-root, half an ounce of cinnamon, and a quarter of an ounce each of cloves and nutmeg. Pound all these very fine, and mix them well with the marrow; then put all into a pewter digester which holds three pints, and let the top be closely fitted. Spread on linen a paste made of flour and white of egg, and fix it over the top so that there can be no evaporation. Suspend the digester by the handles in the middle of a pot of boiling water, and keep it boiling, adding more boiling water as often as necessary. Strain the pomade into small wide-mouthed bottles, and cover it down when quite cold.

479.—*Another Recipe.*

Take three-quarters of a pound of beef marrow; clean it well from bone and fibre, and wash it in water fresh from the spring, which must be changed night and morning for ten days; then steep it in rose-water for twenty-four hours, and drain it. Take half an ounce each of storax, gum benjamin, and odoriferous cyprus-powder, two drachms of cinnamon, and a drachm of cloves. Let these ingredients be all powdered and well mixed with the marrow, and put them in a pewter pot which holds about a pint and a half. Make a paste of white of egg and flour, and lay it on a piece of linen, and place a second linen to cover the pot very tight and keep in the steam. Place the pot in a copper vessel of water, and keep it steady, so that the water may not reach or touch the covering. As the water evaporates, add more, boiling hot, and keep it boiling four hours without ceasing. Strain the pomade into small jars or boules, and cork when quite cold. Take care to touch it only with silver.

480.—Bandoline for the Hair.

Mix two ounces of olive oil with one drachm each of spermaceti and oil of bergamot; heat and strain; then beat in six drops of otto of roses. If colour be desired, add half a drachm of annatto.

481.—Dentifrice.

Scrape as much whiting to a fine powder as will fill a pint pot; moisten two ounces of camphor with a few drops of brandy, rub it into a powder, and mix with the whiting half an ounce of powdered myrrh. Bottle it, and keep it well corked down, taking small quantities out in a separate bottle for daily use.

482.—*Another Recipe.*

Dissolve two ounces of borax in three pints of boiling water; before quite cold, add a teaspoonful of tincture of myrrh and a tablespoonful of spirits of camphor: bottle the mixture for use. One wineglassful of the solution, with half a pint of tepid water, is sufficient for each application. Applied daily, it preserves and beautifies the teeth, extirpates all tartarous adhesion, produces a pearl-like whiteness, arrests decay, and induces a healthy action in the gums.

483.—*Another Recipe.*

No dentifrice in the world can equal that of powdered betel-nut if properly prepared, but very few know how to do this: the nuts should not be burnt, but sliced and roasted, like coffee, to a rich brown colour, and then pulverized and passed through fine muslin; the grit should then be repounded and strained through muslin, and this operation continued until all the powder is finely sifted. The colour, instead of being black, like charcoal, should be a fine rich chocolate-colour. The dentifrice may then be used just as it is, or tincture of myrrh and camphor and eau de Cologne may be added to it.

484.—Rose Lip-salve.

Take an ounce and a half of spermaceti, nine drachms of white wax, twelve ounces of oil of sweet almonds, two ounces of alkanet-root, and one drachm of otto of roses; digest the first four ingredients with the heat of boiling water for four hours, then strain through flannel, and add the otto of roses.

485.—Essence of Roses.

Mix two drachms of otto of roses and a pint of rectified spirits of wine.

486.—Essence of Lemon-peel.

Steep six ounces of lemon-peel, cut very thin and without any particle of the white skin, in eight ounces of spirits of wine well corked.

487.—Eau de Cologne.

Put twelve drops each of oil of neroli, citron, bergamot, orange, and rosemary, and a drachm of cardamom-seeds, into a pint of spirits of wine, and let it stand for a week.

488.—Lavender-water.

Mix two drachms of oil of lavender, half a drachm of oil of bergamot, a drachm of essence of musk, thirteen ounces of spirits of wine, and five ounces of water, and let it stand a week.

MISCELLANEOUS USEFUL RECIPES.

489.—To Unite Broken Glass or China.

Rub the edges of the pieces that require mending with the white of an egg, and then dust some slack lime upon them; hold them together till they stick, and let them dry. This cement is not liable to be softened by heat.

490.—Cement for Attaching Metal to Glass or Porcelain.

Mix two ounces of a thick solution of glue with one ounce of linseed-oil varnish or three-quarters of an ounce of Venice turpentine. Boil together, agitating until the mixture becomes as intimate as possible. The pieces cemented should be fastened together for forty-eight or sixty hours.

491.—Japanese Cement.

This is made by thoroughly mixing rice-flour with cold water, and then gently boiling it; it is beautifully white, and dries almost transparent.

492.—To Clean Silks, Satins, Coloured Woollen Dresses, &c.

Mix well together a quarter of a pound each of soft soap and honey, the white of an egg, and a wineglassful of gin; the article should be scoured thoroughly with rather a hard brush, rinsed in cold water, left to drain, and ironed whilst damp.

493.—To Remove Stains from Mourning Dresses.

Boil a handful of fig-leaves in two quarts of water until reduced to a pint. Bombazines, crape, cloth, &c., need only be rubbed with a sponge dipped in this liquor, and the stains will be instantly removed.

494.—To Remove Ironmould.

Rub the spot with a little powdered oxalic acid, or salts of lemon, and warm water. Let it remain a few minutes, and then well rinse it in clear water.

495.—To Clean Kid Gloves.

First see that your hands are clean; then put on the gloves and wash them, as though you were washing your hands, in a basin of spirits of turpentine, until quite clean; hang them up in a warm place, or where there is a good current of air, which will carry off all smell of the turpentine.

496.—To Clean Feathers.

To every gallon of water allow half a pound of quick-lime; stir the mixture well, and let it stand a night; then pour off the water that is perfectly clear, put the feathers to be cleaned into a deep tub, and pour in as much lime-water as will cover them; let them stand two or three days, stirring them frequently; then put them into a bag, and wash them thoroughly in cold water; turn them out on sieves, and wring the water from them by squeezing them in small portions with the hands, after which they may be separated, the hard quills picked out, and the down stripped from the large feathers. When they are thus carefully cleaned, lay them on a floor where air can be freely admitted; turn and shake them frequently, and when dry, put them into bags, and beat them on a knocking-stone with a knocker.

497.—To Wash Lace.

Place the lace in folds, and baste it on each side; lay it in cold water for a night, and wash it in cold water with the best white soap; gently rub and squeeze it; wash it in three or four waters with the soap, and rinse it well in clean water; then put it into thin starch or rice-water; take out the basting thread, and spread it on a blanket upon a bed to dry; when it is nearly so, pick it out, and lay it in folds, and when quite dry, lay it in an old cambric handkerchief, and then in the folds of a towel; put it upon the rug, or upon a blanket laid upon a stone, and with a heavy wooden pestle, or rolling-pin, beat it hard till it looks quite smooth. A scarf or veil, after being starched, should be pinned out tight upon a cloth on the floor, and when dry, beaten in the same manner.

498.—To Wash Head and Clothes Brushes.

Put a dessertspoonful of pearl-ashes into a pint of boiling water, and shake the brush about in it till it is perfectly clean; then pour some clean hot water over it; shake, and dry it before the fire.

499.—To Clean Gold Chains, Earrings, &c.

Make a lather of soap and water, and boil the chain in it for a few minutes; immediately on taking it out, lay it in magnesia powder which has been heated by the fire, and when dry, rub it with flannel; if embossed, use a brush.

500.—To Clean Plate.

Boil an ounce each of cream of tartar, alum, and common salt in a gallon of water; put the plate in and boil it, and when taken out and rubbed dry it will have a fine polish. Plate, when laid aside, will generally tarnish, but if cleaned by this method at stated periods, it will always look well.

501.—To Clean Marble.

Sift through a fine sieve two parts of common soda, one of pumice-stone, and one of finely-powdered chalk, and mix it with water; rub it well all over the marble, and the stains will be removed; then wash the marble with soap and water, and it will be perfectly clean.

THINGS WORTH KNOWING.

502.—To Make Stale Bread Fresh.

If stale bread be immersed in cold water for a moment or two, and re-baked for about an hour, it will be for the time in every respect equal to newly-baked bread; but the deception will be found out in the course of a few hours.

503.—How to Select and Keep Coffee.

In purchasing coffee, always prefer the Mocha—a small roundish berry of a bluish tint. Never buy it roasted; a coffee-roaster can be procured at a reasonable price, and the trouble of roasting and grinding it at home is not very great. Let it be kept in a plain tin canister, and when roasted and ground transfer it to a smaller air-tight one, as nothing deteriorates coffee so much as exposure to the light and air after it has been roasted.

504.—Lettuce Salad.

Salads should be very fresh, carefully washed, picked, and dried in a clean cloth, cut up separately, and put into the bowl only just before they are required for use. The salad mixture should be placed at the bottom of the bowl and the salad on top; if mixed, the leaves lose that crispness which is so delicious. Slices of beet, eggs, or boiled potatoes are placed on the top to garnish.

505.—Substitute for Cream in Tea or Coffee.

Beat the white of an egg to a froth, and mix well with it a very small lump of butter; then add the coffee to it gradually, so that it may not curdle. If perfectly done, it will be an excellent substitute for cream

506.—*Another Way.*

Beat up, separately, the yolk and white of an egg; transfer them into a large cup, and pour over it sweetened coffee, scalding hot. Skim away the froth, and fill the coffee into a cup of the required size.

507.—To Protect Bed Linen and Curtains from Burning.

Add an ounce of alum to the last water in which the linen and curtains are to be rinsed, and they will be rendered uninflammable, or so slightly combustible that they would take fire very slowly, if at all. This is a simple precaution, and is recommended where there are children and in the sick chamber.

508.—To Prevent the Smoking of a Lamp.

Soak the wick in strong vinegar, and dry it well before using; it will then burn both sweet and pleasant, and give much satisfaction for the trifling trouble in preparing it.

509.—Transparent Paper.

Paper can be made as transparent as glass, and capable of being substituted for many purposes, by spreading over it on both sides, with a feather, a very thin layer of resin dissolved in spirits of wine. Fine thin post paper is the best for the purpose.

510.—To Take Impressions of Leaves.

A very beautiful and cheap way of taking impressions of leaves is to take a small quantity of bichromate of potass (say a teaspoonful), which may be had at any druggist's or colourman's shop; dissolve it in a saucer-ful of water, and pass the paper on which the impressions are to be taken through the solution; while wet press the leaves lightly upon it, and expose it to the sun, which should be shining powerfully. When perfectly dry, remove the leaves, and a perfect facsimile will remain in a light lemon shade, while the rest of the paper will be of a dark brown tint. Bichrome, as it is generally termed, is in dark yellow crystals, which should be powdered previous to using it.

511.—To Take Impressions of Leaves on Silk, &c.

Prepare two rubbers by tying up wool, or any other substance, in wash-leather; then rub up with cold-drawn linseed oil the wished-for colours, as indigo for blue, chrome for yellow, &c.; dip the rubbers into the paint, and rub them one over the other, so that too much may not remain upon them; place a leaf on one of the rubbers and damp it with the other; take the leaf off and apply it to the silk, satin, paper, or other substance you wish stamped; place a piece of paper on the leaf, and rub it gently, and there will be a beautiful impression of all the veins. Leaves can only be used once; they should be all nearly the same size, or the pattern will not look uniform.

INDEX.

FISH.

GARNISHES, SAUCES, STUFFINGS, ETC.

HOME-MADE LIQUEURS.

INDIAN PICKLES, CHUTNEES, SAUCES, ETC.

INDIAN PRESERVES, JAMS, JELLIES, AND MARMALADES.

JOINTS, MADE DISHES, ETC.

MEDICINAL AND OTHER RECIPES.

MISCELLANEOUS USEFUL RECIPES.

PASTRY, PUDDINGS, SWEETMEATS, ETC.

PELLOW OR POOLOO.

PERFUMERY, COSMETICS, AND DENTIFRICE.

RICE OR CHOWL.

SOUPS.

THINGS WORTH KNOWING.

VEGETABLES.

A CATALOGUE

OF

THACKER, SPINK, & CO.'S

PUBLICATIONS.

5 & 6, *GOVERNMENT PLACE,*

CALCUTTA.

A LIST OF

WORKS IN GENERAL LITERATURE,

PUBLISHED OR SOLD BY

THACKER, SPINK, AND CO.,

5 & 6, Government Place, Calcutta.

HISTORY, BIOGRAPHY, POLITICS, &c.

Bellew.—THE RACES OF AFGHANISTAN; being a Brief Account of the principal Nations inhabiting that Country. By Surgeon-Major H. W. BELLEW, C.S.I., late on special Political Duty at Cabul. 8vo., cloth. Rs. 3-8.

Aberigh-Mackay.—THE SOVEREIGN PRINCES AND CHIEFS OF CENTRAL INDIA. By G. R. ABERIGH-MACKAY, Principal, Residency (Rajcoomar) College, Indore, Central India. Illustrated with Portraits and Views. Volume I. Royal 8vo., cloth, extra gilt, and gilt top. Rs. 12.

NOTES ON WESTERN TURKISTAN. Some Notes on the Situation of Western Turkistan. By G. R. ABERIGH-MACKAY. 8vo. Rs. 2-8.

McCrindle.—ANCIENT INDIA AS DESCRIBED BY MEGASTHENES AND ARRIAN; being a Translation of the fragments of the "Indica of Magasthenes" collected by DR. SCWAUBECK and a translation of the first part of the "Indica of Arrian," with Introduction, Notes, and a Map of Ancient India. By J. W. MCCRINDLE, M.A., Principal of Patna College 8vo. Rs. 2-8.

THE COMMERCE AND NAVIGATION OF THE ERYTHRÆAN SEA; being a Translation of Periplus Maris Erythræi by an Anonymous Writer, and of Arrian's Account of the Voyage of Nearkhos from the mouth of the Indus to the head of the Persian Gulf. With Introduction, Commentary, Notes, and Index. By J. W. MCCRINDLE, M.A., Principal of the Government College, Patna. 8vo. Rs. 3.

Sherring.—HINDU TRIBES AND CASTES AS REPRESENTED IN BENARES. Illustrated. By the REV. M. A. SHERRING. 4to., cloth. Rs. 16.

Vol. II. HINDU TRIBES AND CASTES; together with an Account of the Mahomedan Tribes of the North-West Frontier and of the Aboriginal Tribes of the Central Provinces. By the Rev. M. A. SHERRING, M.A., LL.B. Demy 4to., cloth. Rs. 16.

This Volume contains an account of the Tribes of the Punjab and its Frontiers, Central Provinces, and Berar; Bombay Presidency and Frontiers of Scind.

Vol. III. Completing the work, with Index to the whole. *In the Press.*

Wheeler.—EARLY RECORDS OF BRITISH INDIA, a History of Early English Settlements as told in Government Records, old Travels, and contemporary documents down to the rise of British Power in India. By J. TALBOYS WHEELER. Royal 8vo., cloth. Rs. 5.

McMahon.—THE KARENS OF THE GOLDEN CHERSONESE. By LT.-COL. A. R. MCMAHON, F.R.G.S. With Maps. Demy 8vo., cloth. Rs. 12-14.

Mead.—SEPOY REVOLT: its Causes and its Consequences. By H. MEAD. 8vo., cloth. Rs. 4.

Wyllie.—ESSAYS ON THE EXTERNAL POLICY OF INDIA. By W. S. WYLLIE, M.A. Edited, with a Memoir and Notes, by W. W. HUNTER, B.A., LL.D. With Portrait. 8vo. Rs. 10.

Rajendra Lala Mittra.—THE PARSIS OF BOMBAY: a Lecture delivered on February 26, 1880, at a Meeting of the Bethune Society. By RAJENDRA LALA MITTRA, LL.D., C.I.E. 8vo., sewed. Re. 1.

Conran.—AUTOBIOGRAPHY OF AN INDIAN OFFICER. By Major H. M. CONRAN. 8vo., cloth. Rs. 3-8.

Hunter.—THE INDIAN MUSSULMANS. By Dr. W. W. HUNTER. Second Edition. 8vo. Rs. 7-8.

A LIFE OF THE EARL OF MAYO, fourth Viceroy of India. With a Narrative of his Indian Administration. By W. W. HUNTER. 2 vols. demy 8vo. Rs. 17-2.

A STATISTICAL ACCOUNT OF BENGAL. By W. W. HUNTER 20 vols. 8vo., half bound. Price per volume, Rs. 4.

ANNALS OF RURAL BENGAL. By W. W. HUNTER. Fifth Edition. 8vo., cloth. Rs. 12-4.

ORISSA; or, The Vicissitudes of an Indian Province under Native and British Rule. With Engravings and Map. By W. W. HUNTER. 2 vols. demy 8vo., cloth. Rs. 22-8.

Valbezen.—LES ANGLAIS ET L'INDE (nouvelles Etudes). By E DE VALBEZEN. 2 vols. 8vo., stitched. Rs. 9.

Yule.—A NARRATIVE OF THE MISSION sent by the Governor-General of India to the Court of Ava in 1855. With notices of the Country, Government, and People. 70 Illustrations and Maps. By Col. H. YULE. Impl. 8vo., half bound, gilt. Rs. 20.

Briggs.—THE NIZAM: his History and Relations with the British Government. By HENRY GEORGE BRIGGS. With Portrait. 2 vols. 8vo. Rs. 15.

Thorburn.—BANNU; or, Our Afghan Frontier. By S. S. THORBURN, C.S., Settlement Officer. With Map. 8vo., cloth. Rs. 12-14.

Laurie. — SKETCHES OF SOME DISTINGUISHED ANGLO-INDIANS, with an account of Anglo-Indian Periodical Literature By Col. W. F. B. LAURIE. With Portrait of Sir John Kaye. 12mo., cloth. Rs. 3-6.

The Rajatarangini.—KINGS OF KASHMIRA; being a Translation of the Sanskrit Work, Rajatarangini of Kahlana Pandita. By JOGESH CHUNDER DUTT. Small 8vo. Rs. 2.

Smith.—MOHAMMED AND MOHAMMEDANISM: Lectures delivered at the Royal Institution of Great Britain in February and March, 1874. By R. BOSWORTH SMITH. Second Edition, revised, with considerable additions. 8vo., cloth. Rs. 6-2.

Muir.—THE LIFE OF MAHOMET, from Original Sources. By Sir WILLIAM MUIR. New and cheaper Edition, in one vol. With Maps. Demy 8vo., cloth. Rs. 10.

The Original Edition, in four volumes 8vo. Rs. 30.

Haggard.—ENGLAND AND ISLAM. By A. H. HAGGARD, B.C.S 8vo. Re. 1.

Syed Ameer Ali.—A CRITICAL EXAMINATION OF THE LIFE AND TEACHINGS OF MOHAMMED. By SYED AMEER ALI Post 8vo., cloth. Rs. 6-8.

CENTRAL ASIAN QUESTIONS FROM AN EASTERN STAND POINT. 8vo., stitched. Rs. 1 8.

Fytche.—BURMAH, Past and Present. With personal Reminiscences of the Country. By Lieut.-Genl. E. A. FYTCHE. Illustrated. 2 vols 8vo. Rs. 21-8.

Haughton.—CHAREEKAR and Service there with the 4th Goorkha Regiment (Shah Shooja's Force), in 1841. An Episode of the First Afghan War. By Col. HAUGHTON, C.S.I. 8vo., sewed. As. 8.

Goldsmid.—LIFE OF LIEUTENANT-GENERAL SIR JAMES OUTRAM. By MAJOR-GENERAL SIR FREDERIC J. GOLDSMID, CB., K.C.S.I. With Illustrations and Maps. 2 vols. 8vo. Rs. 23.

Malcolm.—A MEMOIR OF CENTRAL INDIA, including Malwa and adjoining Provinces, with the History, and Copious Illustrations, of the past and present conditions of that Country. By MAJOR-GENERAL SIR JOHN MALCOLM, G.C.B., K.L.S. Reprinted from the Third Edition. In two vols. crown 8vo. Rs. .

TRAVELS, GUIDE-BOOKS, &c.

Keene.—A HANDBOOK FOR VISITORS TO AGRA AND ITS NEIGHBOURHOOD. By H. G. KEENE, C.S. Fourth Edition, revised. Maps, Plans, &c. Fcap. 8vo., cloth. Rs. 2-8.

A HANDBOOK FOR VISITORS TO DELHI AND ITS NEIGHBOURHOOD. By H. G. KEENE, C.S. Third Edition. Maps. Fcap. 8vo., cloth. Rs. 2.

A HANDBOOK FOR VISITORS TO ALLAHABAD, CAWNPORE, AND LUCKNOW. By H. G. KEENE, C.S. Second Edition, re-written and enlarged. Fcap. 8vo. Rs.

Ince.—THE KASHMIR HANDBOOK; a Guide for Visitors. With Map and Routes. By JOHN INCE, M.D. Third Edition. Rs. 5.

CALCUTTA TO LIVERPOOL, BY CHINA, JAPAN, AND AMERICA, IN 1877. By H. W. N. Fcap. 8vo., cloth. Rs. 2.

HOW WE DID "THE LIONS" OF THE NORTH-WEST: a Trip in the Durga-Pujahs to Lucknow, Delhi, Agra. By F. O. B. Re. 1.

Bholanath Chunder.—TRAVELS OF A HINDU TO VARIOUS PARTS OF BENGAL AND UPPER INDIA. By BHOLANATH CHUNDER. With an Introduction by J. TALBOYS WHEELER. 2 vols. small 8vo., cloth. Rs. 12.

Stephen. — THE DELHI HANDBOOK. By CARR-STEPHEN. Stitched. Rs. 8.

THE ARCHÆOLOGY AND MONUMENTAL REMAINS OF DELHI. By CARR-STEPHEN. Royal 8vo., cloth. Rs. 10.

Villeroi.—A TRIP THROUGH CENTRAL ASIA. By BERNARD DE VILLEROI. 12mo. Re. 1.

Cornish.—UNDER THE SOUTHERN CROSS. By HENRY CORNISH. Second Edition. Revised, enlarged, and illustrated. 8vo. Rs. 3.

Vaughan.—THE MANNERS AND CUSTOMS OF THE CHINESE OF THE STRAITS SETTLEMENTS. By J. D. VAUGHAN, Barrister-at-Law. 8vo., stiff cover. Rs. 3.

NATURAL AND PHYSICAL SCIENCES.

Clarke.—COMPOSITÆ INDICÆ DESCRIPTÆ ET SECUS GENERA BENTHAMII ORDINATÆ. By C. B. CLARKE, M.A. Demy 8vo. Rs. 1-8.

ROXBURGH'S FLORA INDICA; or, Descriptions of Indian Plants. Reprinted literatim from Carey's Edition. 8vo., cloth. Rs. 5.

Day.—REPORT ON THE FRESH WATER FISH AND FISHERIES OF INDIA AND BURMAH. By J. DAY. 8vo., boards. Rs. 2.

Kurz.—FOREST FLORA OF BRITISH BURMAH. By S. KURZ, Curator of the Herbarium, Royal Botanical Gardens, Calcutta. 2 vols. demy 8vo., cloth. Rs. 15.

Beavan.—HANDBOOK OF THE FRESH WATER FISHES OF INDIA. Giving the characteristic peculiarities of all the Species at present known, and intended as a guide to Students and District Officers. By Capt. R. BEAVAN, F.R.G.S. Twelve full Plates. Demy 8vo. Rs. 7-8.

Theobald.—DESCRIPTIVE CATALOGUE OF THE REPTILES OF BRITISH INDIA. By W. THEOBALD, Geographical Survey. 8vo., cloth. Rs 10.

Nevill.—A CATALOGUE OF MOLLUSCA IN THE INDIAN MUSEUM. By G. NEVILL. Demy 8vo., stitched. Rs 2.

Dobson.—A MONOGRAPH OF THE ASIATIC CHIROPTERA AND CATALOGUE OF BATS IN THE COLLECTION OF THE INDIAN MUSEUM, CALCUTTA. By G. S. DOBSON. Demy 8vo., cloth. Rs. 6.

Gore.—A GLOSSARY OF FOSSIL MAMMALIA. For the use of Students of Palæontology. By J. E. GORE. Fcap. 8vo., cloth. Rs. 1-8.

SOUTHERN STELLAR OBJECTS between the Equator and 55° South Declination. By J. E. GORE. 8vo., cloth. Rs. 2-8.

Jerdon.—THE BIRDS OF INDIA: being a Natural History of all the Birds known to inhabit continental India, a Manual of Ornithology specially adapted for India. By the late T. C. JERDON, to which is added his Supplementary Notes published in the "Ibis." 3 vols. 8vo., cloth. Rs. 30.

Blanford.—THE INDIAN METEOROLOGIST'S VADE MECUM. Part I.—Instructions to Meteorological Observers in India. Part II.—Meteorology of India. With Tables for the reduction of Meteorological Observations in India. By H. F. BLANFORD. 2 Parts, large 8vo., cloth. Rs. 10.

RAINFALL TABLES. Table of Average Monthly and Annual Rainfall in Northern India, &c. One Sheet. As. 4.

McGregor.—PROTECTION OF LIFE AND PROPERTY FROM LIGHTNING DURING THUNDER-STORMS. By W. MCGREGOR. Second Edition, enlarged. Stitched. Re. 1.

Archibald.—THE RAINFALL OF THE WORLD in connection with the eleven-years period of Sunspots. With an Introduction and Appendix. By E. D. ARCHIBALD, B.A., F.M.S. Demy 8vo., stitched. Rs. 2.

Elson.—THE SAILOR'S EAST INDIAN SKY INTERPRETER AND WEATHER BOOK; being a Description of the Phenomena and Prognostics of the Bay of Bengal October-Cylones, as experienced at the Pilot Station off the mouth of the Hooghly. By S. R. ELSON. 8vo. Re. 1.

THE MORSE UNIVERSAL MARINE FLASHING SIGNALS, for use, with the Commercial Code Signal Book in foggy weather, Night Signalling, &c., with a selection of twenty-one handy Night Towing Signals. By S. R. ELSON, Licensed Hooghly Pilot. 8vo., sewed. As. 12.

Yonge.—LATITUDE AND LONGITUDE WITHOUT INSTRUMENTS; being a Chart for finding the Hour of Sunrise and Sunset for every day in the year, at every place in the Northern or Southern Hemisphere. By Capt. W. L. YONGE, R.A. On paper, Re. 1; on India-rubber, Rs. 2-8.

FINANCE, PRODUCE, &c., OF INDIA.

Seyd.—THE FALL IN THE PRICE OF SILVER: its Causes, its Consequences, and their possible Avoidance, with special reference to India. By ERNEST SEYD, F.S.S. 8vo. Rs. 1-12.

Hector.—CURRENCY CONSIDERED WITH SPECIAL REFERENCE TO THE FALL IN THE VALUE OF SILVER AND ITS CONSEQUENCES TO INDIA. By J. HECTOR. 8vo. Pamphlet. Rs. 1-6.

Smeaton.—THE CURRENCY OF INDIA: an Examination of the reasons for change of the present Standard of Value and of the mode of effecting it. By D. MACKENZIE SMEATON, Bengal Civil Service. Demy 8vo., stitched. Re. 1.

Oakeley.—REMARKS ON MR. WILSON'S MINUTE ON THE INTRODUCTION OF A GOLD CURRENCY IN INDIA. By H. E. OAKELEY, M.A. 8vo. Pamphlet. Re. 1.

Lees.—THE DRAIN OF SILVER TO THE EAST, AND THE CURRENCY OF INDIA. By Colonel W. NASSAU LEES, LL.D. Demy 8vo., cloth. Rs. 5.

MEMORANDUM WRITTEN AFTER A TOUR THROUGH THE TEA DISTRICTS IN EASTERN BENGAL IN 1864-65. By Colonel W. NASSAU LEES, LL.D. Rs. 5.

THE LAND AND LABOUR OF INDIA, a Review. By Colonel W. NASSAU LEES, LL.D. 8vo., cloth. Rs. 4.

Smith.—SILVER AND THE INDIAN EXCHANGES; a Remedy for its Depreciation, in seven Essays. By Colonel J. T. SMITH, R.E., F.R.S. Demy 8vo., boards. Rs. 1-8.

Baildon.—TEA IN ASSAM. A Pamphlet on the Origin, Culture, and Manufacture of Tea in Assam, with an Appendix—Rural Life amongst the Assamese. By S. BAILDON. Demy 8vo. Rs. 2.

Hem Chunder Kerr.—REPORT ON THE CULTIVATION OF, AND TRADE IN, JUTE IN BENGAL, and on Indian Fibres available for the Manufacture of Paper. By HEM CHUNDER KERR. Fcap. folio. Paper boards. With Map. Rs. 8.

Hughes.—NOTES ON THE COST OF CARRIAGE BY RAIL AND WATER IN THE UNITED STATES OF AMERICA. With Maps and Statistical Plans. By A. J. HUGHES, C.E. Demy 8vo., boards. Rs. 3-8.

Stoker.—MANAGEMENT OF THE TEA PLANT. By T. STOKER. 8vo., stitched. Rs. 2.

Watson.—REPORTS ON COTTON GINS and on the Cleaning and Quality of Indian Cotton. By D. FORBES WATSON. Part II.—Detailed Description with Records of the Cotton Gin. Trials at Manchester. Dharwar, and Broach (published by order of the Secretary of State for India in Council). Imperial 8vo. Rs.

Digby.—FAMINE CAMPAIGN IN SOUTHERN INDIA (Madras and Bombay Presidencies and Province of Mysore), 1876—78. By WILLIAM DIGBY, Hony. Secy., Indian Famine Relief Fund. Two vols. demy 8vo., cloth. Rs. 16.

Money.—CULTIVATION AND MANUFACTURE OF TEA. By Lieut.-Col. EDWARD MONEY. Prize Essay. Third Edition, corrected and much enlarged. Demy 8vo., cloth. Rs. 5-6.

Hull.—COFFEE PLANTING IN SOUTHERN INDIA AND CEYLON; being a Second Edition, revised and enlarged, of "Coffee," its Physiology, History, and Cultivation. By E. C. P. HULL. 12mo., cloth. Rs. 6.

Schrottky.—MAN, PLANT AND SOIL, AND THEIR CORRELATIONS. By EUGENE C. SCHROTTKY. 8vo., paper. Re. 1.

MILITARY WORKS.

Barrow.—THE SEPOY OFFICER'S MANUAL; a Book of Reference for Officers of the Bengal Native Infantry. By LIEUT. E. G. BARROW, 7th N. I. Pocket. Rs. 2-8.

BENGAL ARMY REGULATIONS. Revised Army Regulations corrected to 1880. Regulations and Orders for the Army of the Bengal Presidency. 8vo., cloth. Rs. 4. Interleaved Copies, Rs. 5.

BENGAL ARMY LIST. The Official Quarterly Army List of H. M.'s Forces in Bengal, exhibiting the Rank, Dates of Commission, and present Location of every Officer in the Bengal Army: to which is added the latest corrected Civil List. Published January, April, July, and October in each year. Each Rs. 4.

Bell.—INSTRUCTIONS IN CAVALRY DRILL. Part III.—Skirmishes, Scouts, Advance, Rear and Flank Guards, Outposts and Patrols. By C. W. BOWDLER BELL. Fcap. 8vo., stiff cover. Rs. 1-12.

PAY CODE. Revised Code of existing Orders regarding Pay, Pension, and Promotion of the Military Services in India. Corrected to 1st May, 1876. Royal 8vo., cloth.

Vol. I.—British Troops, including Officers and Men, Indian Army. Rs. 4.

Vol. II.—Native Troops, including Followers of British and Native Troops. Rs. 2.

Furse.—STUDIES ON MILITARY TRANSPORT. By G. A. FURSE, Major, 42nd Royal Highland Regiment. 8vo., stitched. Rs. 3.

Schmid.—THE SOLDIER IN THE FIELD. A Guide to the Theoretical Instruction of Non-Commissioned Officers and Soldiers in Picquet and Outpost Duties. By Major A. SCHMID. Sewed. Re. 1.

Stubbs.—HISTORY OF THE ORGANIZATION, EQUIPMENT, AND WAR SERVICES OF THE REGIMENT OF BENGAL ARTILLERY. Compiled from Published Works, Official Records, and various private sources, by Colonel FRANCIS W. STUBBS. With numerous Illustrations and Maps. Demy 8vo., cloth. 2 vols. Rs. 23-8.

Trench.—SHORT SERVICE AND DEFERRED PAY. By Captain F. CHENEVIX TRENCH. Second Edition, revised and enlarged. 8vo., stitched. Rs. 2-8.

Voyle.—A MILITARY DICTIONARY, comprising Terms, scientific and otherwise, connected with the Science of War. By Major-General G. E. VOYLE. Third Edition (London, 1876). 8vo. Rs. 7-8.

Broome.—THE RISE AND PROGRESS OF THE BENGAL ARMY. Maps and Plans. By General A. BROOME. Vol. I. (all published). 8vo., cloth. Rs. 5.

TARGET PRACTICE. The Soldiers' and Volunteers' Handbook. How to Shoot straight. 12mo. Rs. 2.

VETERINARY WORKS, SPORTS, &c.

Humfrey.—THE STEEPLECHASE HORSE: how to Select, Train, and Ride Him. With Notes on Accidents and Diseases, and their Treatment. By Capt. J. HUMFREY. Cloth, limp. Rs. 3-8.

Hayes.—VETERINARY NOTES FOR HORSE-OWNERS. With Hindustani Vocabulary; an every-day book. By Capt. M. HORACE HAYES. Illustrated. Crown 8vo. Second Edition, enlarged. [*In the press.*

A GUIDE TO TRAINING AND HORSE MANAGEMENT IN INDIA. With a Hindustanee Stable and Veterinary Vocabulary and Calcutta Turf Club Tables for Weight for Age and Class. By Capt. M. HORACE HAYES, Author of "Veterinary Notes for Horse-Owners." New Edition, re-arranged and much enlarged. Crown 8vo. Rs. 5.

RIDING ON THE FLAT AND ACROSS COUNTRY. Specially directed to Professional Riding of Jockeys and Huntsmen. [*In preparation.*

Baldwin.—THE LARGE AND SMALL GAME OF BENGAL AND THE NORTH-WESTERN PROVINCES OF INDIA. By Capt. J. H. BALDWIN. With numerous Illustrations. 4to., cloth. Rs. 15.

Kinloch.—LARGE GAME SHOOTING IN THIBET AND THE NORTH-WEST. By Capt. ALEX. A. KINLOCH, C.M.Z.S., 60th Royal Rifles. Illustrated by Photo. tint. Second Series, in demy 4to., cloth, gilt. Rs. 15.

Sterndale.—SEONEE; OR, CAMP LIFE ON THE SAPTURA RANGE. A Tale of Indian Adventure. By ROBERT A. STERNDALE, F.R.G.S. Illustrated by the Author. Demy 8vo. Rs. 15.

DOMESTIC ECONOMY AND MEDICINE.

Birch.—GOODEVE'S HINTS FOR THE MANAGEMENT AND MEDICAL TREATMENT OF CHILDREN IN INDIA. By EDWARD A. BIRCH, M.D., Surgeon-Major. Seventh Edition. Crown 8vo., cloth. Rs. 7.

"I have no hesitation in saying that the present one is for many reasons superior to its predecessors. It is written very carefully, and with much knowledge and experience on the author's part, whilst it possesses the great advantage of bringing up the subject to the present level of Medical Science." [Dr. Goodeve.

THE INDIAN COOKERY BOOK: A Practical Handbook to the Kitchen in India, adapted to the three Presidencies; containing original and approved Recipes in every Department of Indian Cookery; Recipes for Summer Beverages and Home-made Liqueurs; Medicinal and other Recipes; together with a variety of things worth knowing. By A THIRTY-FIVE YEARS' RESIDENT Crown 8vo. Rs. 3.

Riddell.—INDIAN DOMESTIC ECONOMY AND RECEIPT BOOK. With Hindustani Names. By Dr. R. RIDDELL. Eighth Edition. Royal 12mo. Rs. 6.

Firminger.—A MANUAL OF GARDENING FOR BENGAL AND UPPER INDIA. By T. A. C. FIRMINGER, Honorary Member, Agri.-Horti. Society. Third Edition. 8vo., cloth, gilt. Rs. 10.

GOODEVE'S HINTS FOR THE GENERAL MANAGEMENT OF CHILDREN IN INDIA in the absence of Professional Advice. Entirely re-written by JOSEPH EWART, M.D. Limp cloth. Rs. 2.

Duke.—QUERIES AT A MESS TABLE: What shall we eat? What shall we drink? By JOSHUA DUKE, Surgeon, 3rd Punjab Cavalry, Author of "Banting in India." Fcap. 8vo., cloth, gilt. Rs. 2-4.

HOW TO GET THIN; or, Banting in India. By J. DUKE. 12mo., stiff cover. Re. 1.

Fullerton.—THE FAMILY MEDICAL GUIDE, with Plain Directions for the Treatment of every Case, and a List of Medicines required for any Household. By GEORGE FULLERTON. Second Edition, revised and improved. 8vo., cloth. Rs. 7-8.

Balfour.—MANUAL FOR NURSES IN INDIA. By Dr. E. BALFOUR. Second Edition. Fcap. 8vo., cloth. Rs. 2.

Hogg.—PRACTICAL REMARKS CHIEFLY CONCERNING THE HEALTH AND AILMENT OF EUROPEAN FAMILIES IN INDIA, with special reference to Maternal Management and Domestic Economy. By FRANCIS R. HOGG, M.D., Surgeon-Major. Demy 8vo., boards. Rs. 2.

Hunter.—MEDICAL HINTS FOR THE DISTRICTS, AND COMPANION TO THE DISTRICT MEDICINE CHEST, arranged for Government Officials, their Families, and Camp-followers, and for all who are cut off from oral Medical Advice. By GEORGE YEATES HUNTER, Surgeon, Bombay Army. Fcap. 8vo., cloth. Rs. 3-8.

HEALTH IN INDIA; Medical Hints as to who should go there; how to retain Health there and on returning Home. By GEORGE YEATES HUNTER. 16mo., cloth, gilt. Rs. 2.

MEDICAL WORKS.

Russell.—THEORY OF MALARIA AND INJURIES OF THE SPLEEN. By E. G. RUSSELL, M.B., B.S.C., London. Demy 8vo., cloth, gilt. Rs. 8.

Hall.—CAUSES OF BLINDNESS IN INDIA, Treatment and Cure, with an Appendix on Hypermetropia, Diagnosis, &c. By Surgeon GEOFFREY C. HALL, Indian Medical Service. Fcap. 8vo., cloth, gilt. Rs. 2.

Roy.—THE CAUSES, SYMPTOMS, AND TREATMENT OF BURDWAN FEVER: or, The Epidemic Fever of Lower Bengal. By GOPAUL CHUNDER ROY, M.D., F.R.C.S., London (Exam.) 8vo., cloth. Rs. 3-6.

Dutt.—THE MATERIA MEDICA OF THE HINDUS. Compiled from Sanscrit Medical Works by UDOY CHAND DUTT; with a Glossary of Indian Plants, by G. KING, M.B., F.L.S. Demy. 8vo., cloth. Rs. 6.

Ranking.—HIDAYAT-UL-HUKUMA. A Hindustani Manual for the use of Indian Medical Officers, Native Doctors, and others. By George S. A. Ranking, B.A., M.B., Cantab., Surgeon, 6th Bengal Cavalry. 18mo., sewed. Rs. 1-4.

Barnard.—CHOLERA MALIGNA is a Specific Acute Inflammation of the Mucous Tissue of the Small Intestines. By G. Barnard. 8vo. Pamphlet. Re. 1.

Billing.—THE NATURE AND TREATMENT OF ASIATIC CHOLERA. By Archibald Billing. 12mo. Re. 1.

THE INDIAN ANNALS OF MEDICAL SCIENCE. Nos. XXVIII to XXXVII., January, 1877. Rs. 4 each.

Munro.—LEPROSY. By W. Munro, M.D., C.M. 8vo., boards. Rs. 3-4.

Chevers.—A PRACTICAL TREATISE ON THE MANAGEMENT OF THE DISEASE OF THE HEART AND OF AORTIC ANEURISM, with especial reference to the Treatment of those Diseases in India. By Dr. Norman Chevers. Demy 8vo., cloth. Rs. 2-8.

Bose.—PRINCIPLES OF RATIONAL THERAPEUTICS, commenced as an Inquiry into the relative value of Quinine and Arsenic in Ague. By Bholanath Bose, M.D. Crown 8vo. Rs. 3-4.

A NEW SYSTEM OF MEDICINE, entitled Recognizant Medicine or, The State of the Sick. By Bholanath Bose. 8vo. Rs. 7-8.

O'Shaughnessy.—THE BENGAL DISPENSATORY. Compiled chiefly from the works of Roxburgh, Wallich, Royle, Ainslie, Wight, Arnoll, Pereira, Fee, Richard, and Lindlay, including the Results of numerous Special Experiments. By W. B. O'Shaughnessy. Large 8vo., cloth. Rs. 8.

Martin.—THE NATURE OF THE TISSUE-CHANGE KNOWN AS FATTY DEGENERATION OF THE HEART. By J. Martin, Medical Department. 8vo., cloth. Re. 1.

Playfair.—A TREATISE ON THE SCIENCE AND PRACTICE OF MIDWIFERY. By W. S. Playfair, M.D. 2 vols. 8vo. Rs. 20.

Ram Narain Dass.—A MONOGRAPH OF TWO HUNDRED AND FORTY-EIGHT CASES OF LATERAL LITHOTOMY OPERATIONS performed in the North-Western Provinces during a period of twelve years, by Ram Narain Dass. Illustrated by 256 Diagrams of Calculi, showing exterior and section, executed in Lithography. Pp. viii., 94. 8vo., cloth. Rs. 10.

Robson.—HOMŒOPATHY EXPOUNDED AND EXPOSED: a Lecture. By W. Robson, M.D. 8vo. As. 8.

SURVEYING.

Thuillier.—MANUAL OF SURVEYING FOR INDIA. Detailing the mode of operations on the Trigonometrical, Topographical, and Revenue Surveys of India. By Col. H. L. THUILLIER and Col. SMYTH. Revised and enlarged. Royal 8vo., cloth. Rs. 12.

Scott.—NOTES ON SURVEYING. For the use of Schools. By J. MIDDLETON SCOTT, C.E. Second Edition. 8vo., stitched. Re. 1.

Kelly.—HANDBOOK OF PRACTICAL SURVEYING FOR INDIA. Especially designed as a Guide and Book of Ready Reference for District Officers, Planters, Municipalities, Courts of Wards, and Landholders and for the use of Surveying Classes. Illustrated with Plans, Diagrams, &c. By F. W. KELLY. Second Edition. Rs. 6.

THEOLOGICAL.

Welland.—EARTHLY AND HEAVENLY TRAINING; Sermons preached to the Calcutta Volunteers. By Rev. JAMES WELLAND. Paper, sewed. Re. 1.

Banerjee.—THE ARYAN WITNESS; or, The Testimony of Aryan Scriptures in Corroboration of Biblical History and the Rudiments of Christian Doctrine, including Dissertations on the Original Home and Early Adventures of Indo-Aryans. By Rev. K. M. BANERJEE. 8vo., paper, Rs. 3-4; cloth, Rs. 4.

DIALOGUES ON THE HINDU PHILOSOPHY, comprising the Nyaya, the Sankhya, the Vedant; to which is added a discussion of the authority of the Vedas. By Rev. K. M. BANERJEE. 8vo., cloth. Rs. 5.

The same freely rendered into Bengalee. 8vo., cloth. Rs. 3-8.

Macdonald.—THE VEDIC RELIGION; or, The Creed and Practice of the Indu-Aryans, three thousand years ago. By the Rev. K. S. MACDONALD, M.A. 8vo., pp. 164, sewed. Rs. 1-8.

Slater.—GOD REVEALED. An Outline of Christian Truth, being Sunday Afternoon Lectures delivered to Educated Hindus. By Rev. T. E. SLATER, London Mission, Madras. Re. 1.

Temple.—THE LORD'S PRAYER TRANSLATED INTO THE BOJINGIJIDA, or South Andaman Language. By E. H. MAN. With Preface, Introduction, and Notes by Lieut. R. C. TEMPLE. 21st R. N. B. Fusiliers. Demy 8vo., cloth. Rs. 3-8.

Long.—SCRIPTURE TRUTH IN ORIENTAL DRESS; or, Emblems Explanatory of Biblical Doctrines and Morals. With Parallel or Illustrative References to Proverbs and Proverbial Sayings in the Arabic, Bengali, Canarese, Persian, Russian, Sanskrit, Tamil, Telegu, and Urdu Languages. By Rev. J. LONG. Half bound Re. 1.

POETRY AND MISCELLANEOUS LITERATURE.

Aliph Cheem.—LAYS OF IND; Poems, Grave and Gay. Sixth Edition, enlarged, with additional Poems and Illustrations by the Author. Cloth, gilt. Rs. 7.

"BASIL ORMOND," and "Christabel's Love:" Metrical Tales of English Life. By ALIPH CHEEM, Author of "Lays of Ind." Rs. 3-8.

THE MEMOIR OF THE LATE JUSTICE ONOOCOOL CHUNDER MOOKERJEE. A Verbatim reprint. 12mo. Rs. 1 8.

Ghose.—LIBERAL EDUCATION IN INDIA. A Paper read at a Meeting of the Bethune Society on the 21st March, 1878. By NAGENDRA NATH GHOSE, Barrister-at-Law. 8vo., sewed. Re. 1.

INDIAN VIEWS OF ENGLAND: the Effects of Observation of England upon Indian Ideas and Institutions. By NAGENDRA NATH GHOSE. Demy 8vo., stitched. Re. 1.

Long.—THREE THOUSAND BENGALI PROVERBS AND PROVERBIAL SAYINGS ILLUSTRATING NATIVE LIFE AND FEELING AMONG RYOTS AND WOMEN. By Rev. J. LONG. 12mo., paper. As. 8.

Maine.—THE EFFECTS OF OBSERVATION OF INDIA UPON MODERN THOUGHT. By Sir HENRY SUMNER MAINE, K.C.S.I., LL.D., the Rede Lecture, 1875. 8vo. Re. 1.

Dutt.—A VISION OF SUMERU AND OTHER POEMS. By SHOSHEE CHUNDER DUTT. With Portrait of the Author. 8vo., cloth. Rs. 5.

Mookerjee.—DURGESA NANDINI; or, THE CHIEFTAIN'S DAUGHTER. A Bengali Romance by BANKIM CHANDRA CHATTERJEE. Translated into English Prose by CHARU CHANDRA MOOKERJEE. 8vo., cloth Rs. 2-8.

STORIES OF THE INDIAN OPERAS. 8vo., stitched. Rs. 2.

Tawney.—TWO CENTURIES OF BHARTRIHARI. By C. H. TAWNEY, Professor, Presidency College, Calcutta. 12mo., cloth. Rs. 2.

Sterndale.—THE AFGHAN KNIFE By ROBERT ARMITAGE STERNDALE, F.R.G.S., Author of "Seonee, or Camp Life on the Satpura Range." Post 8vo. Rs. 4-4.

LIFE IN THE MOFUSSIL; or, The Civilian in Lower Bengal. By an EX-CIVILIAN. 2 vols. Rs. 10.

Mitchell.—IN INDIA. Sketches of Indian Life and Travel from Letters and Journals. By Mrs. MURRAY MITCHELL. Sq. 16mo., cloth. Rs. 2-8.

Day.—GOVINDA SAMANTA; or, The History of a Bengal Ryot. By the Rev. LAL BEHARI DAY. Crown 8vo. Rs. 4-4.

Grant.—RURAL LIFE IN BENGAL, illustrative of Anglo-Indian Suburban Life; the Habits of the Rural Classes; the varied Produce of the Soil and Seasons, and the Culture and Manufacture of Indigo. By C. GRANT. Illustrated with 166 Engravings. Royal 8vo., cloth. Rs. 6-8.

ANGLO-INDIAN DOMESTIC LIFE. By the Author of "Rural Life in Bengal." Profusely illustrated, A new Edition abridged and re-written with the Original and other Illustrations selected by the late COLESWORTHY GRANT. [*In preparation.*

DIRECTORIES, EXAMINATION MANUALS, TABLES, &c.

THACKER'S BENGAL DIRECTORY, Comprising, amongst other information, Official Directory; Military Directory; Mofussil Directory; Commercial Directory; Trades Directory; Street Directory, Calcutta; Alphabetical List of Residents in Bengal Presidency. Seventeenth Annual Publication. Royal 8vo., cloth, Rs. 14 cash; Rs. 16 credit.

BENGAL OBITUARY; a Compilation of Tablets and Inscriptions; with Directory, Biographical Sketches, and Memoirs. Royal 8vo., cloth Rs. 6.

CIVIL LIST FOR THE LOWER PROVINCES OF BENGAL. Published quarterly. Rs 3.

CALCUTTA UNIVERSITY CALENDAR, containing the Acts incorporating the University and authorizing it to grant Degrees—Bye-Laws—Regulations for all the Examinations, with lists of subjects and Text-Books—The University List of Fellows, Affiliated Institutions, Graduates, &c., and Papers set at the last Examinations in all Degrees, Demy 8vo., cloth. Rs. 5.

Grimley.—RULES FOR THE DEPARTMENTAL EXAMINATIONS OF JUNIOR MEMBERS OF THE COVENANTED CIVIL SERVICE, the Subordinate Executive Service, the Non-Regulation Commission, Police and Opium Departments; including a Selection of Examination Papers, in which are incorporated specimens of questions in Bentham's Theory of Legislation, Political Economy, History of India. For the Examination of Candidates for admission into the Staff Corps, and of Officers in the Political Department. By W. H. GRIMLEY, C S., Secretary to the Central Examination Committee. 8vo., boards Rs. 5.

GUIDE TO THE SUBORDINATE CIVIL SERVICE EXAMINATIONS, including a Selection from the Questions set in previous Examinations and the Orders of Government on the subject. By W. H. GRIMLEY. 8vo., boards. Rs. 4.

THE HUNDRED YEARS' ANGLO-CHINESE CALENDAR, from 1776 to 1876. 8vo., stitched. Rs. 7.

Jarrett.—A MANUAL OF REFERENCE TO THE EXAMINATIONS IN ORIENTAL LANGUAGES HELD THROUGHOUT THE BENGAL PRESIDENCY, containing the latest Orders of Government of India, establishing the Tests for Civil and Military Officers, Graded Officers of the Educational Department, and of the Uncovenanted Service, with Specimens of Test Papers for the various Examinations. By H. S. JARRETT, Secretary to the Board of Examiners. Stitched. Rs. 2-8.

Tables.

Merces.—TABLES OF EXCHANGE. A New Edition, showing the Conversion of English Money into Indian Currency and *vice versa*, calculated for every 16th of a Penny, from 1*s*. 5*d*. to 2*s*. 3*d*. per Rupee. By F. A. D'MERCES. 8vo. Rs. 8.

TABLES OF INTEREST, showing the Interest of any sum from 3 pie to 100,000 rupees, at any rate from 1 to 15 per cent. per annum, reckoning 360 and 365 days to the year. By F. A. D'MERCES. New Edition. Demy 8vo., bound. Rs. 4.

TABLES OF INCOME, WAGES, RENTS, &c., for months of 28, 29, 30, and 31 days; from 4 annas to 10,000 rupees, advancing by 1 rupee to 100 rupees. By F. A. D'MERCES. Fcap. 8vo. Rs. 1-4.

THE HANDY CALCULATOR, showing the cost of goods by Number, per dozen, per hundred, per pound, per maund, and at so many seers and chittacks per rupee; also containing Tables of Income, Wages, &c., and Weights. By F. A. D'MERCES. 12mo., pp. 264. Rs. 3.

Spens.—THE INDIAN READY-RECKONER. Containing Tables for ascertaining the value of any number of Articles, &c., from 3 pies to 5 rupees, also Tables of Wages, from 4 annas to 25 rupees, and other useful Tables. By Capt. A. T. SPENS. Rs. 1-12.

Todivala.—MERCHANTS' AND BANKERS' COMPANION; or, Tables for calculating Interest and Commission, Freight and Exchanges between India, England, and China, in Rupees, Sterling, and Dollars. With Tables to show the Rates of Exchange and Prices of Bullion. By MANEKJI KAVASJI TODIVALA Royal 8vo. Rs. 12.

THE LANGUAGES OF INDIA.

Hindustani.

ARAISH-I-MAHFIL. Printed in Urdu. For the use of the Junior Members of Her Majesty's Indian Civil and Military Services. Fourth Edition. Revised and corrected by W. NASSAU LEES, LL.D. 8vo., paper. Rs. 6.

FISANAH-I-AJAIB OF MIRZA ALI BEG SURUR. New and Revised Edition. For Examination for Degrees of Honour in Urdu. 8vo. Rs. 4.

Lower Standard. — HINDUSTANI SELECTIONS FOR THE LOWER STANDARD EXAMINATION; being Selections from the Bagh-o-Bahar and History of India. 8vo. Rs. 2-8.

Higher Standard.—HINDUSTANI SELECTIONS FOR THE HIGHER STANDARD; being Selections from the Bagh-o-Bahar and Premsagur. 8vo., stitched. Rs. 4-8.

IKHWAN-US-SAFA, IN URDU. Fourth Edition, revised and corrected. For Examination, High Proficiency in Urdu. 8vo. Rs. 3.

NUZR-I-BE-NUZEER, IN URDU. Third Edition, revised and corrected. For Examination, High Proficiency in Urdu. 8vo. Rs. 3.

NAZR-I-BI-NAZIR. Translated from Urdu by C. W. BOWDLER BELL. 8vo., stitched Rs. 4-8.

NAZR-I-BI-NAZIR; or, The Incomparable Prose of Meer Hussen. Literally translated by Capt. M. H. COURT. 8vo., stitched. Rs. 5-8.

Stapley.—GRADUATED TRANSLATION EXERCISES. Part II—English-Urdu, Urdu-English. With Rules, and Remarks for the guidance and assistance of Native Teachers and Students. By L. A. STAPLEY. 8vo., paper. Ans. 6.

KULLIYAT-I-SAUDA OF MIRZA RAFI-US-SAUDA, Extracts from, in Urdu. For Examination for Degrees of Honour in Urdu. 4to. Rs. 4.

MUSNAWIYAT OF MIRZA RAFI-US-SAUDA. For Candidates for the High Proficiency Examination in Urdu. Sewed. As. 12.

Court.—SELECTIONS FROM THE KULLIYAT-I-SAUDA. The parts appointed for the High Proficiency Examination. Literally translated by Capt. M. H. COURT. 8vo., paper. Rs. 3.

Yates.—INTRODUCTION TO THE HINDUSTANI LANGUAGE. Eighth Edition, improved. By Rev. W. YATES. In Roman Character, Rs. 5. In Persian Character, Third Edition, Rs. 6.

URDU ENTRANCE COURSE. Selections appointed by the Calcutta University. Poetry, As 12; Prose, As. 10.

Jarrett.—TRANSLATION OF THE HINDU PERIOD OF MARSHMAN'S HISTORY for the Lower Standard Examination. By Major H. S. JARRETT. 8vo. Rs. 1-4.

Bell.—THE RAJNITI OF LALLU LALA. Translated from the Braj Bhasha by C. W. BOWDLER BELL. 8vo., stitched. Rs. 6.

BYTAL PACHEESEE; or, The Twenty-five Tales of a Demon. Reprinted from the New Edition of Eshwar Chandra Vidyasagar in Hindi. Second Edition. Rs. 3.

Thompson.—A DICTIONARY IN HINDI AND ENGLISH. Compiled from approved Authorities. Second Edition. By J. T. THOMPSON. Royal 8ov., paper. Rs. 10.

Sanscrit.

Tawney.—UTTARA RAMA CHARITTA, a Sanscrit Drama by Bhavabhute. Translated into English Prose by C. H. TAWNEY, Professor, Presidency College, Calcutta. Sewed. Rs 1-8.

THE MALAVIKAGNIMITRA: a Sanscrit Play by Kalidasa. Literally translated into English Prose by C. H. TAWNEY, Professor, Presidency College, Calcutta. 12mo., cloth. Rs. 2.

TWO CENTURIES OF BHARTRIHARI. By C. H. TAWNEY, Professor, Presidency College, Calcutta. 12mo., cloth. Rs. 2.

Banerjee.—BHUTTI KAVYA: Poem on the Actions of Rama. The first five Books, with Notes and Explanations. By Rev. K. M. BANERJEE. 8vo., paper. Rs. 2.

KUMAR SAMBHAVA OF KALIDASA. With Notes and Explanations in English. By Rev. K. M. BANERJEE. Third Edition, revised. 8vo., paper. Rs. 2-8.

RAGHUVANSA BY KALIDASA. With Notes and Grammatical Explanations. By Rev. K. M. BANERJEE. 8vo., paper. No. 1 (Cantos 1—3), Rs. 2. No. 2 (Cantos 4—9), Rs. 3. The two parts together, Rs. 4.

Ram Jasan.—A SANSCRIT AND ENGLISH DICTIONARY; being an abridgment of Professor Wilson's Dictionary. With an Appendix explaining the use of Affixes in Sanscrit. By PANDIT RAM JASAN. Royal 8vo., cloth. Rs. 10.

WILSON'S DICTIONARY IN SANSCRIT AND ENGLISH; translated, amended, and enlarged from an original Compilation prepared by learned Natives for the College of Fort William. Third Edition. By JAGUN MOHANA TARKALANKA and KHETTER MOHANA MUKERJEE. 4to., bound. Rs. 16.

Persian.

A'ARAS-I-BOZORGAN; being an Obituary of Pious and Learned Moslims, from the beginning of Islam to the Middle of the 12th Century of the Hijirah. Edited in Persian by Col. W. N. LEES and KABIR ALDIN AHMED. 8vo, paper. Rs. 2-8.

GULISTAN OF SADY. Edited in Persian, with Punctuation and the necessary Vowel-marks. Third Edition, revised and corrected. By Col. W. N. LEES. For Examination, High Proficiency in Persian. 8vo. Rs. 5.

IQD-I-GUL; being a Selection from the Gullistan and Anwari Sohaili. For Examination, Higher Standard. Rs. 3.

IQD-I-MANZUM; being a Selection from the Bostan of Sadi. Edited by KABIR ALDIN AHMED. Second Edition. For Examination, Higher Standard. 8vo. Rs. 2.

SELECTIONS FROM THE SHAH NAMAH. For the Degree of Honor Examination in Persian. For Officers in the Military and Civil Services. By Major H. S. JARRETT. Published by Authority.

Lees's Persian Series :—

I.—ZAWABIT-I-FARSI ; or, A Persian Grammar in Oordoo. Prepared by ABD-UL-HUQQ. Seventh Edition. 12mo. As. 5.

IV.—IQD-I-LAALI ; or. A Persian Poetical Reader, No. 1, containing the Pand-Nama or Karima and the Tarjiband, called Mamoquiman. Second Edition. 12mo. As. 4.

V.—IQD-I-MARJAN ; or, Persian Poetical Reader, No. 2, containing the Pand-Nama of Farid Aldin Attar and the Quiccah-i-Yoosof ; being an extract from Jami's Poem Yoosof and Zalaikha. Second Edition. 8vo. As. 8.

MODERN PERSIAN PHRASES. By an Officer of the Hyderabad Contingent. Revised by AKA MIRZA ZENUL ABIDEES SHEERAZEE. 8vo., cloth. Rs. 5.

PERSIAN SELECTIONS FOR FIRST ART COURSE, Rs. 1-4 ; For B. A. Course, Rs. 2-8.

Arabic.

ALIF LAILA (THE) ; or, Book of the Thousand Nights and one Night. Edited by Sir W. H. MACNAGHTEN. 4 vols. royal 8vo., (all remaining copies soiled). Rs. 25.

ARABIC SELECTIONS FOR THE ENTRANCE EXAMINATION entitled Sullam-ul-Adah. 8vo., cloth. Rs. 3-8.

ARABIC SELECTIONS FOR THE FIRST ARTS EXAMINATION, 8vo., cloth. Rs. 2-8.

Hayes.—SYNOPSIS OF THE GRAMMAR OF MODERN ARABIC. With a Vocabulary and Dialogues. By Capt. F. F. C. HAYES. Fcap. 8vo., paper. Rs. 2.

KALUBI, IN ARABIC. Edited by Col. W. N. LEES and MAULAVI ABD-UL-HUQQ. 8vo. Rs. 2.

KASHAF ; being the Commentary on the Koran. By ABL-KASIM MUHMAD. 2 vols. 4to. Rs. 25.

Lees's Arabic Series :—

I.—ARABIC INFLECTION. 12mo. As. 4.
II.—ARABIC SYNTAX. 12mo. As. 4.
III.—TUHFAT-UL-TALIBIN. 12mo. As. 4.

Pukshto.

Bellew.—A DICTIONARY OF THE PUKHTO OR PUKSHTO LANGUAGE. In which the words are traced to their sources in the Indian and Persian Languages. By H. W. BELLEW. 4to., cloth. Rs. 21.

A GRAMMAR OF THE PUKHTO OR PUKSHTO LANGUAGE on a new and improved system, combining brevity with practical utility, and including Exercises and Dialogues intended to facilitate the acquisition of the Colloquial. By H. W. BELLEW. 4to., cloth. Rs. 10-8.

Vaughan.—A GRAMMAR OF THE PUKSHTO LANGUAGE as spoken in the Trans-Territories under British Rule. By Capt. J. L. VAUGHAN. 8vo., paper. Rs. 4.

Bengali.

STAPLEY'S GRADUATED TRANSLATION EXERCISES adapted to the Bengali Language. 8vo. As. 8.

THE LITERATURE OF BENGAL, from the earliest times to the present day. By ARCYDAE. With Extracts. 12mo., stitched. Re. 1.

Mendes.—ABRIDGMENT OF JOHNSON'S DICTIONARY, English and Bengali. 2nd Edition. By JOHN MENDES. 8vo., cloth. Rs. 5.

YATES'S INRODUCTION TO THE BENGALI LANGUAGE. Edited by J. WENGER. Vol. I.—Grammar and Reader, 8vo., cloth. Rs. 5; Vol. II.—Selection from Bengali Literature. 8vo. Rs. 5.

Glossaries.

Carnegy. — KACHARI TECHNICALITIES; or, A Glossary of Terms—Rural, Official, and General—in daily use in the Courts of Law, and in illustration of the Tenures, Customs, Arts, and Manufcatures of Hindustan. By P. CARNEGY. Demy 8vo., cloth. Rs. 12.

Durga Prasad.—A GUIDE TO LEGAL TRANSLATION; or, A Collection of Words and Phrases used in the Translation of Legal Papers from Urdu to English. By DURGA PRASAD. 8vo., cloth. Rs. 5.

Rajendra Lala Mittra.—A SCHEME FOR THE RENDERING of European Scientific Terms into the Vernacular of India. By RAJENDRA LALA MITTRA. Demy 8vo., stitched. As. 8.

Robinson.—DICTIONARY OF LAW AND OTHER TERMS commonly employed in the Courts of Bengal, including many Commercial Words and Idiomatic Phrases, in English and Bengali. By JOHN ROBINSON. 8vo. Rs. 6.

EDUCATIONAL WORKS.

Including Macmillan & Co.'s English Series of "Text books for Indian Schools" (English prices at the Exchange of the day).

ENGLISH LANGUAGE.

MILTON'S ODE ON THE MORNING OF CHRIST'S NATIVITY. With Notes (Todd's). Fcap. 8vo., limp. As. 4.

A GUIDE TO ENGLISH PARSING. By H. P. JACOB. Fcap. 8vo. As. 4.

LAMB'S TALES FROM SHAKESPEARE. Thacker, Spink, & Co.'s School Edition. Fcap., cloth. As. 12.

SELECTIONS FROM MODERN ENGLISH LITERATURE. By E. LETHBRIDGE. 8vo., cloth. Rs. 2.

FIRST ARTS COURSE FOR 1881. Authorized by the Calcutta University. 8vo., cloth. Rs. 5.

ENGLISH CLASSICS FOR INDIAN SCHOOLS: Goldsmith's Deserted Village. Edited by G. W. FORREST and STORR. As. 12.

EASY SELECTIONS from Modern English Literature. By E. LETHBRIDGE. 1*s.* 6*d.*

A SERIES OF SIX ENGLISH READING-BOOKS. For Indian Children. By PEARY CHURN SIRCAR. Revised by E. LETHBRIDGE. First, 5*d.*; Second, 6*d.*; Third, 8*d.*; Fourth, 1*s.*; Fifth, 1*s.* 2*d.*; Sixth, 1*s.* 3*d.*

HINTS ON THE STUDY OF ENGLISH. By F. J. ROWE and W. T. WEBB. Demy 8vo., cloth. Rs. 2-8.

A COMPANION READER to "Hints on the Study of English." Demy 8vo., paper. Rs. 1-4.

THE STUDENT'S COMPANION TO ENGLISH GRAMMAR. Compiled from University Examination Papers. By J. TANNOCK, Nizamut College, Moorshedabad. 8vo., stitched. As. 8; Supplement, 1876.

A KEY TO TANNOCK'S STUDENT'S COMPANION TO ENGLISH. By G. A. LORRIMER. 8vo., sewed. As. 8.

ENGLISH PEOPLE AND THEIR LANGUAGE. Translated from the German of Loth by C. H. TAWNEY. Stitched. As. 8.

A PRIMER OF ENGLISH GRAMMAR. For Indian Students. By the Rev. R. MORRIS, M.A., LL.D. 1*s.*

A SHORT HISTORY OF ENGLISH LANGUAGE. By THOMAS EDWARDS, F.E. Fcap. 8vo. Rs. 1-4.

GEOGRAPHY.

A GEOGRAPHICAL READER AND COMPANION TO THE ATLAS. By C. B. CLARKE, M.A. 2*s.*

PHYSICAL GEOGRAPHY. For Indian Students. By H. F. BLANFORD, Associate of the Royal School of Mines, Director-General of the Indian Meteorological Department. 2*s.* 6*d.*

HISTORY.

THE WORLD'S HISTORY. Compiled under the direction of E. LETHBRIDGE, M.A. Second Edition. 1*s.*

AN EASY INTRODUCTION TO THE HISTORY OF INDIA. Second Edition. By E. LETHBRIDGE, M.A. 1*s.* 6*d.*

A HISTORY OF ENGLAND. Second Edition. Compiled under the direction of E. LETHBRIDGE, M.A. 1*s.* 6*d.*

AN EASY INTRODUCTION TO THE HISTORY AND GEOGRAPHY OF BENGAL. Second Edition. By E. LETHBRIDGE, M.A. 1*s.* 6*d.*

MATHEMATICS.

EUCLID'S ELEMENTS OF GEOMETRY. Part. I., containing the First Four Books, with Notes, &c. By P. GHOSH. Sewed, Rs. 1-4 ; cloth, Rs. 1-8.

A CHAPTER OF DECIMALS. By J. M. ALDIS, M. A. 16mo., stitched. Re. 1.

ARITHMETIC FOR BEGINNERS, designed for the use of Junior Classes, to which are appended Exercises in Mental Arithmetic. By CHARLES D'CRUX, Bengal Academy. 16mo. As. 6.

SOLUTIONS OF EXERCISES FROM TODHUNTER'S MENSURATION. Including Surveying, and an Appendix. By P. GHOSH. 12mo. Rs. 1-8.

ELEMENTARY TREATISE ON MECHANICS. By F. W. STEPHENSON. Stitched, 8vo. Rs. 2-8.

ARITHMETIC WITH ANSWERS. For Indian Students. By BARNARD SMITH, M.A. 2*s.*

This Edition of Barnard Smith's Arithmetic contains the Indian Tables of Weights, Measures, and Currency, as well as the English Tables; and Examples fully worked out, and very numerous Questions for practice, based on the Tables, have been inserted under each rules.

ALGEBRA. For Indian Students. By I. TODHUNTER, M.A., F.R.S. 2*s*. 6*d*.

THE FIRST FOUR BOOKS OF EUCLID. With Notes, Appendix, and Exercises. By I. TODHUNTER, M.A., F.R.S. 2*s*.

ELEMENTARY MENSURATION AND LAND SURVEYING. For Indian Students. By I. TODHUNTER, M.A., F.R.S. 2*s*.

This Edition of Todhunter's Mensuration has been prepared specially for Entrance Candidates, and contains an Appendix on Practical Surveying in India.

NOTES ON PRACTICAL GEOMETRY AND THE CONSTRUCTION OF SCALES. By J. M. SCOTT. 2nd Edition. 8vo., stitched. Re. 1.

THE ELEMENTS OF ALGEBRA, by JAMES WOOD; remodelled, simplified, and adapted for general use in schools, with numerous Exercises and Examination Papers. Part I. For Entrance Candidates. By P. GHOSH. 12mo., cloth. Rs. 1-8.

MISCELLANEOUS ARITHMETICAL QUESTIONS selected from various sources. With neat and concise Solutions. By EDWARD FELL. 12mo. Rs. 2.

ELEMENTARY TREATISE ON PLANE TRIGONOMETRY. With Examination Papers and Examples. Designed for the use of the Government Colleges of India, and Schools affiliated to the University of Calcutta. By E. WILMOT. Pp. 76. 8vo., cloth. Rs. 2-12.

ALGEBRAICAL EXERCISES WITH SOLUTIONS. For Students preparing for the Entrance Examination of the Calcutta University. By SARAT CHANDRA MUKHOPADHYAY, M.A. 12mo., stiff cover. Rs. 1-4.

ELEMENTARY DYNAMICS, with numerous Examples. By W. G. WILLSON. Second Edition, by J. WILLSON. Crown 8vo. Rs. 3-8.

BENGALI.

BENGALI ENTRANCE COURSE. Entrance Examination. Rs. 1-6.

THE WORLD'S HISTORY. Compiled under the direction of E. LETHBRIDGE, M.A. Translated into Bengali. Demy 8vo. As. 8.

AN EASY INTRODUCTION TO THE HISTORY AND GEOGRAPHY OF BENGAL. For the Junior Classes in Schools. By E. LETHBRIDGE, M.A. Translated into Bengali. Demy 8vo. Re. 1.

A PRIMER OF CHEMISTRY. By H. E. ROSCOE. Translated into Bengali. Demy 8vo. As. 8.

STAPLEY'S GRADUATED TRANSLATION EXERCISES, adapted to the Bengali Language. As. 8.

ELEMENTS OF EUCLID. First two Books. With Notes and Exercises. Translated into Bengali. Demy 8vo. As. 6.

MENSURATION FOR BEGINNERS. With numerous Examples. By I. TODHUNTER, M.A., F.R.S. Translated into Bengali. Demy 8vo. As. 12.

EXTRACTED CHAPTERS FROM THE RUDIMENTS OF PHYSICAL GEOGRAPHY FOR INDIAN SCHOOLS. By H. F. BLANFORD Translated into Bengali by BABOO PURNA CHANDRA DATTA for the Author. As. 10.

AN EASY INTRODUCTION TO THE HISTORY OF INDIA. By E. LETHBRIDGE, M.A. Translated by BABOO RADHIKA PRASANNA MUKERJEE. Demy 8vo. Re. 1.

METAPHYSICS.

THE ELEMENTS OF THE PSYCHOLOGY OF COGNITION. By R. JARDINE. Crown 8vo. *6s. 6d.*

ANALYSIS OF SIR WILLIAM HAMILTON'S LECTURES ON METAPHYSICS, with Dissertations and Copious Notes. By W. CAREY FINK, Author of an "Analysis of Dr. Thos. Reid's Inquiry into the Human Mind." Rs. 2.

ANALYSIS OF REID'S INQUIRY INTO THE HUMAN MIND. By W. C. FINK. With Notes. 8vo., stitched. Rs. 1-8.

LECTURES ON METAPHYSICS. By Sir WILLIAM HAMILTON, Bart. 2 vols. 8vo., cloth. Rs. 9.

AN INQUIRY INTO THE HUMAN MIND ON THE PRINCIPLES OF COMMON SENSE. By THOMAS REID, D.D. 8vo., cloth. Rs. 1-4.

LATIN.

SELECTA POETICA. The Selection adopted by the Calcutta University. Part I., Selections from Ovid. 18mo., cloth. Re. 1 Translation. Re. 1.

SELECTA POETICA. The Selections adopted by the Calcutta University. Part II., Selections from Cartullus, Tibullus, Propertius, Martial, Aulus, Persius, Juvenal. 18mo., cloth. Re. 1. Translation. Re. 1.

ARNOLD'S ECLOGŒ OVIDIANÆ. A Translation. Fcap. 8vo., sewed. Re. 1.

INDIAN LAW PUBLICATIONS.

Civil Procedure.

Code of Civil Procedure (The); being Act X of 1877. With Notes, and Appendix, containing Charters of all the High Courts, Privy Council Appeals, Orders, Rules, The Limitation and Specific Relief Acts; with Copious Index. By L. P. DELVES BROUGHTON, assisted by W. F. AGNEW and G. S. HENDERSON. Royal 8vo. Reduced to Rs. 18.

Evidence.

The Law of Evidence (Act I of 1872, with Amendments). With a Commentary, Notes, &c. Third Edition. By C. D. FIELD. Demy 8vo., cloth. Rs. 18.

Contracts.

The Indian Contract Act (IX of 1872). With a Commentary, critical, explanatory, and illustrative. By C. C. MACRAE. 8vo., cloth. Rs. 10.

The Indian Contract Act (IX of 1872), and the Specific Relief Act (I of 1877). With a full Commentary. By D. SUTHERLAND. Royal 8vo., cloth. Rs. 10.

The Contract Act (IX of 1872). With an Introduction and Explanatory Notes. By the Hon. H. S. CUNNINGHAM, M.A.,and H. H. SHEPHARD, M.A. Third Edition. Demy 8vo., cloth. Rs. 14.

Criminal Law.

The Code of Criminal Procedure (Act X of 1872), and other Laws relating to the Procedure in the Criminal Court of British India. With Notes and Abstracts of the Interpretations by the High Courts. Fifth Edition. By H. T. PRINSEP, C.S. Cloth. With addenda. Royal 8vo. Rs. 16.

The Indian Penal Code (Act XLV of 1860), and other Laws and Acts of Parliament relating to the Criminal Courts of India. With Notes containing the Rulings of the Nizamut Adawlut on points of Procedure and Decisions of the High Court of Calcutta. By J. O'KINEALY. Second Edition. Royal 8vo. Rs. 14.

The Indian Magistrate's Guide: an Introduction to the Judicial Duties of Magistrates and Justices of the Peace in India. By Sir Benson Maxwell. Edited for India by L. P. Delves Broughton, B.A., Barrister-at-law. 8vo., cloth. Rs. 12.

The Penal Code, Act XLV of 1860 (Fifth Edition), as amended by later Enactments. With Rulings of all the High Courts and Chief Courts in India. By Fendall Currie. 8vo., cloth. Rs. 8.

The Indian Code of Criminal Procedure. With Rulings of all the High Courts in India and the Chief Courts of the Provinces. With a copious Index. (Fifth Edition.) By Fendall Currie. 8vo., cloth. Rs. 10-8.

Pocket Penal, Criminal Procedure, and Police Codes: Acts XLV of 1860, X of 1872, V of 1861, VI of 1864, XXXI of 1867, and XXVII of 1870. Limp cloth. Rs. 4.

Divorce.

The Law of Divorce in India; being the Indian Divorce Act. With Notes and forms of Pleading. By C. C. Macrae. Cloth. Rs. 10.

Insolvency.

The Law and Practice of Insolvency in India, being 11 and 12 Vict., cap. 21. With Notes and Rules and Orders of the High Courts of Calcutta, Madras, and Bombay. By Henry Millett and Frederick Clarke. Cloth, 8vo. Rs. 8.

Joint Stock Companies.

The Indian Companies' Act, 1866 (Act X of 1866). With an Appendix and Notes. By Whitley Stokes. Royal 8vo. Rs. 8.

Succession.

The Indian Succession Act, 1865 (Act X of 1865). With a Commentary, and the Parsee Succession Act, 1865, Acts XII and XIII of 1855, and the Acts relating to the Administrator-General. With Notes. By Whitley Stokes. 8vo. Rs. 10.

Mortgages.

Law of Mortgage in Bengal and the North-West Provinces. By A. G. MACPHERSON, Judge of the High Court of Judicature. Sixth Edition. Demy 8vo. Rs. 10.

Registration.

The Indian Registration Act (III of 1877). With Notes (fourth edition of the Notes). By CARR-STEPHEN, Barrister-at-Law. Demy 8vo., cloth. Rs. 5.

Landlord and Tenant.

The Rent Law of Bengal, L. P. (Act VIII, 1869, B.C.). with all important Rulings and Notes. By JOGINDRA CHANDRA MAULIK. 8vo., cloth. Rs. 7-8.

The Law of Landlord and Tenant as administered in Bengal. By H. BELL, C.S. Second Edition. Cloth, large 8vo. Rs. 7-8.

Miscellaneous.

The Indian Law Examination Manual. Second Edition Revised with all the new Laws. By FENDALL CURRIE. 8vo. Rs. 5.

The Sea-Customs Law, 1878, and Tariff Act; with Notes and Appendices. By W. H. GRIMLEY, Esq., B.A., LL.B., C.S. Demy 8vo., cloth, Rs. 7-8; Interleaved, Rs. 8-8.

Legislative Acts.

Bengal Acts: the Legislative Acts (Unrepealed) of the Lieutenant-Governor of Bengal in Council. From 1862 to the present. Annotated and edited, with Index, by FRED. CLARKE, Esq., Barrister-at-Law. Rs. 22.

Legislative Acts published annually in continuation of Mr. Theobald's Edition. Royal 8vo., cloth—1872, Rs. 8; 1873, 1874, 1875, Rs. 5 each; 1876, Rs. 6; 1877, Rs. 10; 1878, Rs. 5; 1879, Rs. 5.

Reports.

Indian Law Reports, published under Authority. The Reports appear in Monthly Parts, at Calcutta, Madras, Bombay, and Allahabad, and comprise four Series,—the Cases heard by the Privy Council on appeal from each High Court are reported in the Series for that High Court. Annual Subscription, Rs. 47-8.

Judgments of the Privy Council on Appeals from India. 1831 to 1877. By D. SUTHERLAND. In paper cover, Rs. 16. Vol. II, 1868 to 1877, Rs. 20. The two vols. together, Rs. 30.

Digests.

The Indian Digest: a complete Index to the Reported Cases of the High Courts established in India. Second Edition. By H. COWELL, Barrister-at-Law. Royal 8vo., cloth. Reduced to Rs. 12.

The Digest of Indian Law Reports: a Compendium of the Rulings of the High Court of Calcutta from 1862, and of the Privy Council from 1831 to 1876. By D. SUTHERLAND, Esq., Barrister-at-Law. Impl. 8vo. Rs. 20.

A Digest of the Cases reported in the Bengal Law Reports, 1868 to 1875. By J. V. WOODMAN, Barrister-at-Law. Royal 8vo., cloth. Rs. 16.

Tagore Law Lectures.

The Hindu Law; being a Treatise on the Law administered exclusively to Hindus by the British Courts in India. (1870.) By HERBERT COWELL. Royal 8vo., cloth. Rs. 12.

The Hindu Law; being a Treatise on the Law administered exclusively to Hindus by the British Courts in India. (1871.) By HERBERT COWELL. Royal 8vo., cloth. Rs. 8.

History and Constitution of the Courts and Legislative Authorities. (1872.) By HERBERT COWELL. Royal 8vo., cloth. Rs. 8.

Mahomedan Law; a Digest of the Laws applicable to the Sunnis of India. (1873.) By SHAMA CHURN SIRCAR. Royal 8vo., cloth. Rs. 9.

Mahomedan Law; being a Digest of the Sunni Code in part, and of the Imamyah Code. (1874.) By SHAMA CHURN SIRCAR. Royal 8vo., cloth. Rs. 9.

The Law relating to the Land Tenures of Lower Bengal. (1875.) By ARTHUR PHILLIPS. Royal 8vo., cloth. Rs. 10.

The Law relating to Mortgage in India. (1876.) By RASH BEHARI GHOSE. Royal 8vo., cloth. Rs. 10.

The Law relating to Minors in Bengal. (1877.) By E. J. TREVELYAN. Royal 8vo., cloth. Rs. 10.

The Hindu Law of Marriage and Stridhana. (1878.) By GOOROO DOSS BANERJEE. Royal 8vo., cloth. Rs. 10.